State of Opera

Music, songs and singing have occupied the larger share of Elizabeth Silsbury's life as long as she can remember. She has worked as teacher, lecturer, conductor, repetiteur and critic for more than four decades, and has held influential positions in many arts organisations, including the first Music Board of the Australia Council (1973–76), Board of the Australian Opera (1977–94) and South Australian education and government funding bodies (1979–98). Her reviews and features are published in local, interstate and overseas newspapers and journals. She holds the degrees of BA and BMus (Hons) from the University of Adelaide and the Elder Conservatorium and Life Memberships of the University of Adelaide Theatre Guild and the Adelaide Chorus. Her love of opera began with playing piano arrangements of Verdi, Mozart and Sullivan as a child, burgeoned into performances of Katisha and the Duchess of Plaza Toro in the Tivoli Theatre as a student at Adelaide Teachers' College, drew her into negotiations setting up New Opera of SA in 1972 and led to her decision in 1995 to write *State of Opera*. She lives in Adelaide and has two daughters and six grandchildren. In 1985 Elizabeth was awarded the OAM for services to music and music education.

State of Opera

An intimate new history of
The State Opera of South Australia
1957–2000

Elizabeth Silsbury

Wakefield
Press

To the memory of Kathleen Steele Scott, without whom this story would be completely different, and would not be written by me.

Elizabeth Silsbury

Wakefield Press
17 Rundle Street
Kent Town
South Australia 5071

First published 2001

Designed and typeset by Clinton Ellicott, Wakefield Press
Printed and bound by Hyde Park Press, Adelaide

National Library of Australia
Cataloguing-in-publication entry

Silsbury, Elizabeth.
State of opera: an intimate new history of
The State Opera of South Australia 1957–2000.

Bibliography.
Includes index.
ISBN 1 86254 555 3.

1. State Opera of South Australia – History.
2. Opera companies – South Australia. I. Title.

982.109943

Wakefield Press thanks The State Opera of South Australia and
Arts South Australia for their assistance in the production of this book.

❧

𝒞ontents

❧

Foreword

$\mathcal{S}$*tate of Opera* records the history of The State Opera of South Australia from 1957 to 2000. It is entirely fortuitous that its publication celebrates the twenty-fifth anniversary of the company's establishment as a statutory authority. In the years leading up to 1976, when Don Dunstan secured the future of opera in South Australia by state legislation, the company metamorphosed from the Intimate Opera Group to New Opera SA, thence to The State Opera. Devotees associated with the early days of constant struggle to make ends meet, especially the redoubtable Kathleen Steele Scott, had the satisfaction of seeing their pioneering work rewarded with artistic achievements second to none in Australia, culminating in the history-making performances of Wagner's *Ring* cycle in 1998.

The idea of a book documenting progress from amateur to professional status had been around for some time, but only in 1995 did the project take shape. Elizabeth Silsbury, who had a long association with opera, both at state and national levels, took up the challenge with patience and dedication after retiring from her position as Senior Lecturer in Music at Flinders University. Moral support was freely available, but it was not until 1998, when Elizabeth was able to secure research grants from Flinders, that work began in earnest. Financial backing from the board of State Opera, from individuals and from ArtSA enabled the manuscript to be completed by December 2000.

I welcome this valuable addition to the growing collection of books documenting the arts history of South Australia. Most appropriately, the publication of *State of Opera* coincides with another landmark in the eventful life of State Opera – the first fully staged Australian production of *Parsifal*.

Len Amadio AM, 2001

1

Prelude

The story told in the opening chapters of this book has all the elements of a grand opera. There is a cast of distinctive characters, all enjoying a great love affair with opera and finding personal fulfilment and excitement in putting on opera. Dressing up in borrowed clothes and hats, improvising sets and collecting props, organising rehearsals and performances, finding places to stage them, packing up trucks with all the clobber for country tours, training and accompanying singers – many of whom were unable to read music at all, let alone fluently – selling tickets, running lotteries and lunches to fund productions or pay off deficits incurred – they laid the foundations of an enterprise that would never have survived without them. And all at their own expense.

There were many attempts to establish regional opera companies in South Australia. All except one came unstuck after a handful of productions. The reasons why Intimate Opera Group (IOG) survived as an amateur family-and-friends enterprise for 15 years, and how it transmogrified into New Opera South Australia in 1973 and thence to The State Opera of SA three years later, are outlined in this book. As in any good opera, some mysteries remain. No explanations will ever adequately account for the determination that kept IOG going in spite of small audiences, electric curtains that opened when they shouldn't and didn't when they should, pianos that played three semitones below normal concert pitch, theatres with appalling acoustics and a bus driver who always lost his keys.

During my preparation of this manuscript there was no dearth of funny stories to flesh out the programs, press cuttings and photographs lovingly preserved by the founders and early members of IOG. Putting together facts and figures about budgets – how they were drawn up, how deficits were met – was considerably more difficult; these matters were obviously of secondary importance to the serious business of 'putting on opera'. Records of expenditure were kept by IOG President Kathleen Steele Scott in Kathleen's cashbook, a tiny Fortis Memo noting costs of items from August 1961 – '£30 spent' – to August 1972 – '$71.63 carried forward'. Documents were carried around in a Kraft cheese box, which served as the office.

The history of IOG would be remarkable in its own right. But when the plot unfolds to reveal how these humble beginnings developed into a fully fledged professional company – one that has established a record unbeaten in this country for presenting major premières, especially of contemporary operas, that was the first in Australia able to meet the monumental demands of putting on *Der Ring des Nibelungen*, and kept moving to mount the Australian première of *Parsifal* – the true value of IOG's contribution to South Australia's operatic supremacy is revealed. And the story does not stop there. In 2004 State Opera will mount a new *Ring*, whose total production will be initiated from within the company.

There are gaps in the story. There would be a lot more, but for the collections and memories of William and Laura Harrison, John Worthley, Kay Gallant, Mary Handley, Rae Cocking, Len Amadio, Justin Macdonnell, and especially Kathleen Steele Scott. Her generosity realised a dream of Douglas Anders to document South Australia's operatic past, and also resulted in an oral history comprising interviews with nine of the early players. The books she supported, *Through the Opera Glass, A Chronological Register of Opera Performed in South Australia 1836 to 1988* (1991), its *Supplement* (1997) and *Intimate Opera Group Oral History* (1999) have been my most fruitful written resources.

From 1973 the more orderly documentation procedures of succeeding professional managements replaced Kathleen's cashbook and the Kraft cheese box, making my task more straightforward, but I remained heavily reliant on the memories of Ian D. Campbell, Hugh and Margaret Cunningham, Richard Brown, David and Alan Farwell, Thomas Edmonds, Myer Fredman, Moffatt Oxenbould, David Kram, Dean Patterson, and many others.

My first acquaintance with IOG was as a member of the audience at their debut production in October 1957, *Three's Company*. Fifteen years later, through my involvement as repetiteur in the Flinders and Adelaide Universities' production of *Pygmalion*, I was drawn into the negotiations leading to the development of the government-funded New Opera of South Australia, and served on its various committees as well as working as repetiteur, chorus director and assistant conductor over several years. In 1977 I began reviewing for local, interstate and overseas publications, and I have supported the company as critic and feature writer ever since.

This book is the culmination of five years of formal investigations, but more than four decades of first-hand experience of the events herein described.

It also celebrates the 25th anniversary of The State Opera's proclamation as a statutory body by the government of South Australia in 1976.

I hope that someone will follow my example for the next 25 years; and the next, and the next . . .

Elizabeth Silsbury, Adelaide, 2001

2

Three's Company:

Intimate Opera Group, 1957–71

The Intimate Opera Group (IOG) was initiated, and named, by singers. Not by administrators, nor politicians, but one bass, one soprano and a tenor. And it was another tenor who suggested the title.

With no other motive than fulfilling their own operatic aspirations, these three, plus a pianist, set in train a process that led directly and continuously to the formation of The State Opera of South Australia (SOSA), today a thriving company, admired nationally and internationally by audiences and critics. Never one to allow its small size to inhibit its aspirations, it mounted the first Australian-based *Der Ring des Nibelungen* in 1998, and in doing so achieved a goal sought by much larger and more prestigious companies.

In 1957 William Harrison, Jaqueline Talbot and John Worthley were members of the Adelaide Singers, the last of what had been a network of Australian Broadcasting Corporation chamber radio choirs in all states of Australia. Between 1946 and 1957 the two men had performed in operas produced at the University of Adelaide's Elder Conservatorium, the former in *Don Giovanni*, in Rutland Boughton's choral drama *Bethlehem* and Debussy's *L'Enfant Prodigue* and the latter in *Faust*, *The Barber of Seville*, *Così fan tutte*, *Carmen*, and *Don Pasquale*.

Of the beginning of IOG William Harrison recalls that John Worthley's brother Max (an Adelaide tenor who returned after many years of working in England to teach at the Elder Conservatorium during the years 1954 to 1958), had received from his friend, the English composer Anthony Hopkins, a copy of his new one-act opera *Three's Company*, hoping that it might be suitable for performance by Max's students. Knowing that his brother John had operatic aspirations and little opportunity for realising them, Max passed the score on to him with the suggestion that he and his friend William Harrison should form their own company and put on the Hopkins opera, an eternal triangle comedy, office style, set to a witty text by Michael Flanders. He also suggested that they should take as their model the Intimate Opera Company (IOC), with which Max had worked in London.

The outcome was the formation of Intimate Opera Group, the name being registered in 1957. The foundation members were the three singers named above and Welsh pianist Eira West, who was working in Adelaide. According to William and Laura Harrison, 'The Intimate Opera Company gave us a guideline for what little bit we knew. It used small casts, piano accompaniment and no props. This served as a good start for a small opera company.'

The IOC was in truth an appropriate model. An English company established in 1930 by Frederick Woodhouse with the specific aim 'to revive unknown opera of the chamber music genre', its public life began with the 1760 opera buffa *Thomas and Sally* by Thomas Arne. Later the IOC commissioned a number of chamber operas from English composers, among them *Three's Company* by English composer Anthony Hopkins, who became the Company's musical and artistic director in 1953.

This highly accessible comedy chose itself for the Adelaide debut of the Intimate Opera Group, and played for a four-night season in October 1957 in Willard Hall in Wakefield Street, Adelaide. The one-act opera was complemented by a short recital from the Cecilia Singers, a group of conservatorium students conducted by Margaret Taverner, who as Margaret Lambert played for several IOG productions in later years.

Conservatorium singing teacher Barbara Howard, well-known to all three singers, began her long and fruitful association with IOG as their director, and the (very simple) sets were designed by Stan Ostoja-Kotkowski, an artist who had recently emigrated from Poland and had offered his services after reading advance publicity in the local newspaper. Eira West directed the music from the piano.

William Harrison's wife Laura worked on front-of-house for *Three's Company*, beginning her long association with the company and its successors.

Three's Company was well received by both press and public. An unsigned review (*Advertiser*, 3 October 1957) referred to IOG's 'unmistakeably successful debut'. The cast was commended for 'singing the music – modern and often quite difficult – splendidly' and for giving 'an exhibition of accomplished comedy action such as one seldom sees in local opera'. C.B. de Boehme observed (*News*, 3 October 1957) that 'The group has made a good start, and it will be interesting to see them in a more representative offering'. Tibor Paul, Acting Conductor, SA Symphony Orchestra, wrote to the Editor (*Advertiser*, 5 October 1957), praising *Three's Company* as a 'first-class musical performance and a most amusing entertainment'. He was one of several writers to complain that 'half the seats were empty'. Following his letter the final performance attracted a full house and the budget was balanced. A special showing of IOG's debut production was mounted at the Studio Theatre, Wellington Square on 17 November for the Elizabethan Theatre Trust Opera Company (ETTOC), which was then playing at the Theatre Royal in Adelaide. In the audience were Max Worthley, playing Rodolfo in *La Bohème*, and his Mimi, Australian soprano Elsie Morrison.

Many years later John Worthley reported in a letter to the editor (*Advertiser*, 22 October 1991) that IOG's first effort was 'an instant success, being broadcast nationally by the ABC, and the four original members being flown to Melbourne to present it on television there'.

According to William Harrison there was no particular concern about the finances of the season. There was no question of any of the participants being paid, the piece was in modern dress, and the fairly minor costs of hall hire and materials for the set were covered 'out of our own pockets'. He himself provided the gear for the sound effects, and expenses, which they agreed to share along with profits, were covered by box office income.

They did it for fun, motivated more by their own love of the stage and desire to perform than by any high-minded principles of supporting and developing the artistic life of the city. Maybe this was the secret, the reason why IOG survived for fifteen years, playing more than 20 operas, most of them from the twentieth century, with virtually no public subsidy, supported primarily by the goodwill and enthusiasm of their company members and audiences.

William Harrison,
Albert Herring, 1958

Two weeks after the *Three's Company* season, Adelaide dance teacher Joanne Priest mounted Benjamin Britten's *Let's Make an Opera* (a mere eight years after its Aldeburgh première in 1949) with her company, the Young People's Theatre, based on her dance studio. Cast as Britten's Miss Bagot in the Priest production was recent arrival, Kathleen Steele Scott. An Englishwoman with a lifelong passion for music and opera, she came to Adelaide in 1936 to marry surgeon Dr John Steele Scott. When John Worthley, playing Clem (as had his brother Max in the opera's première in Aldeburgh in 1949), stated his interest in having IOG produce Britten's *Albert Herring,* Kathleen Steele Scott encouraged him by revealing that she had seen the opera in London and had brought the score back to Adelaide.

John Worthley's and IOG's next move was a production of *Herring* in the Union Hall at Adelaide University in October 1958. Again, less than a decade separated the Adelaide season from the work's première in Aldeburgh, Sussex.

In addition to the three founding singers of IOG, the cast included Kathleen Steele Scott, Barbara Howard, Joan Gill, Lillian Siggs, Leslie Dutton, Kingsley Payne and Neville Hicks, most of whom became IOG regulars. J.V. Peters, Senior Lecturer in Music at the Elder Conservatorium and Organist and Master of Choristers at St Peter's Cathedral, conducted the orchestra comprising members of the South Australian Symphony Orchestra, and the designer was local theatre identity Tom Steel. Kathleen Steele Scott played the maid Florence, but is also credited as the producer. She recalled, 'When the originally scheduled producer Hedley Cullen withdrew, I said I'd like to have a go, so I did produce it, in a hand-to-mouth sort of way'.

At this time subsidies were unknown. If you wanted to put on an opera, you paid for it, and as *Herring* was scored for twelve players and mounted in a professional theatre, its costs were considerable. Kathleen Steele Scott remembered that 'We all put in £100 to pay for *Herring*, hoping for a return, but of course we all lost money'.

A savvy publicist would have capitalised on the plot, an English variation on Guy de Maupassant's story about a village search for a virgin to play Queen of the May. The choice settles not on a maid, because there aren't any, but a man, the hapless and apparently gormless Albert. But in 1958 opportunities for promotion were practically non-existent, and none of the IOG had the requisite skill and nous. Audiences were very, very small.

The reviews were generally favourable. Not surprisingly, the critics found the music 'odd' and 'intriguing'. Harold Tidemann (*Advertiser*, 14 October 1958) noted that 'The Opera, in its modern idiom, is entirely different to anything presented here before', and rated the overall result as 'very meritorious'. James Govenlock (*Sunday Mail*, 18 October) declared that IOG had 'scored a winner'.

The Group had also scored a winner with the elegant, imperious Englishwoman whose first name, Kathleen, rapidly became its unofficial trade-mark, a guarantee of quality and innovation.

Information about the financial details of these early productions is scanty, as IOG existed from opera to opera, rather than as a continuous organisation, and there was little reason to keep records of expenditure and income once a season was over. From August 1961 notes on IOG purchases were kept in a little Fortis Memo book known as 'Kathleen's cashbook', but no documentation of *Herring's* money matters has been found.

Although the performances of Britten's farce-with-a-twist could have been ranked as being of a professional standard, the running of the company, and especially the book-keeping, was entrusted to members whose competencies in these matters was rather more amateur. Laura Harrison recalled that Kathleen Steele Scott handled the finances (often meaning that she paid for things herself), and that Mrs Williams, the secretary of her husband Dr John Steele

Scott, looked after the accounts and kept a running budget. According to the same source, *Herring* lost a lot of money.

IOG's next venture was relatively modest. Menotti's *The Telephone* and Arthur Benjamin's *Prima Donna* played for four nights, 24–27 June 1959, in Willard Hall. William Harrison, Marie Bates, Trevor Rodger and Noel Robbins sang major roles, Alison Holder and Shirley Sawtell conducted from the piano, Stan Ostoja-Kotkowski and Toni Graham were the designers, and Kathleen Steele Scott and Hedley Cullen directed. Between the two operas, Walter Gore's short ballet *Peep Show* was produced by Cecil Bates for the SA Repertory Ballet. The program for this event listed six members of the production team, headed by accountant Doris Brokensha named as Treasurer.

James Govenlock (*Sunday Mail*, 27 June 1959), commended the show and wrote that 'The Intimate Opera Group has further enhanced its reputation' with the two operas. In *Australian Theatre Year* (1959/60), the normally extremely-hard-to-please Max Harris set the IOG in an Adelaide context. 'In a city like Adelaide, professionally pathetic but almost over-endowed with amateur groups, transcendent occasions occur quite often … During the past year

John Worthley, Noel Robbins and William Harrison, *Prima Donna*, 1959

there have been one or two productions of this kind. The most notable has been the work of the Intimate Opera Group, a collection of first-class singers … whose infectious élan has brought a neglected idiom to abundant life in Adelaide.' He described the June season as 'an unquestioned triumph'.

Although nominally John Worthley was the prime mover in IOG's event throughout the 1958 and 1959 productions, Kathleen Steele Scott's natural leadership qualities became gradually more evident. Without making any obvious moves, she began to assume a more prominent role in the Group's affairs, making a formidable pair with Barbara Howard. Soprano Rae Cocking was quite in awe of them. Forty years on from her first engagement with IOG, she still treasures the memory of these two tall, well-built women striding together down North Terrace deep in conversation, complete with their white gloves, flowered hats and sensible shoes, looking like Margaret Rutherford and Joyce Grenfell about to change the world.

In September 1959 IOG mounted a return season of *Three's Company*, again in tandem with the South Australian Repertory Ballet. A letter to the editor and a review (*Sunday Mail*, 10 October) both referred to the small audiences. The letter-writer (F.M. Seaton Park) wrote, 'In a city like Adelaide, with a developing musical and theatrical tradition, it is surprising and rather disquieting that a production of this merit should play to half-empty houses', and the reviewer, Nadra Penalurick, noted that 'the response of Adelaide's so-called interested opera patrons is appalling'.

1960 was an extremely active year for IOG, comprising three city seasons and four separate tours which took them to five different country towns.

In March (during, but not officially associated with, the first Adelaide Festival of Arts) came *The Telephone, The Scarf* (Lee Hoiby) and Lennox Berkeley's *A Dinner Engagement*. Singers Rae Cocking, Ian Giles and Janice Hearne (later Chapman) and pianists Dorothy Oldham and John Chapman joined IOG for these works, which were directed by Barbara Howard.

The season comprised eleven performances in Mead Hall in the city's Flinders Street, four at night and seven during lunch hours. They found favour with the local critics, and also with visitor Martin Long, who wrote in the Sydney *Daily Telegraph* that the works were 'stylishly produced'. Just as well he was not aware that John Worthley's distress as his wife Rae Cocking strangles him with the scarf she has been knitting during the interminable Russian winter was not entirely simulated: he had in fact swallowed a bit of his false beard and was actually choking. He made a speedy exit.

Given that most of the cast had day jobs, the density of this run was truly remarkable. Laura and William Harrison described how members of the Adelaide Singers would finish their rehearsals at 12.30 pm at the ABC in Hindmarsh Square, 'shoot round to the theatre' several blocks away, be ready to start at ten past one, play their parts and be back at their jobs 'just after two, provided the conductor turned a blind eye'.

Prior to this season in March 1960 IOG had established a structure. The program names Lady Bonython as Patroness, Kathleen Steele Scott as President, John Worthley as Secretary to an Executive Committee comprising Jacqueline Talbot, William Harrison and Barbara Howard, and Joan Gill as Treasurer. At this time the company apparently felt that there was no need to enlist the services of anyone with business or legal experience, believing that the singers themselves were capable of dealing with all aspects of the operations. In matters relating to rehearsing and mounting productions this confidence was justified, but advice from outside the performers' circle might have assisted in attracting a wider audience, and hence brought more order to the financial dealings.

The popularity of the lunch-hour and evening programs in March 1960 can be largely attributed to them taking place during the inaugural Adelaide Festival of Arts (AFA), when a general mood of artistic interest and enthusiasm was engendered, but audiences were not similarly attracted to subsequent seasons of similar repertoire.

Soprano Margaret MacPherson made the first of many appearances for IOG in August with seven performances in Mead Hall of *Susanna's Secret* by Wolf-Ferrari, this being the first IOG collaboration by Conservatorium colleagues Barbara Howard (director) and Alison Holder (musical director). Critic Mark Taylor (*Advertiser*, 26 August 1960) held up the 'style and attention to detail of the sets and costumes' of *Susanna's Secret* as 'an example to all our amateur theatre groups.' But the heroine would not have been a good example for health. Suzanna is a closet smoker, not a philandering wife, and all ends happily with everyone merrily puffing away. Of course they did not inhale.

Just as IOG had taken everything else in its stride, the company seems to have embarked on an extensive country tour without too many reservations about the complex logistics involved. The three one-act pieces of the Adelaide Festival of Arts program were trundled around Maitland (8 July), Booleroo Centre (3 September) – where the scenery became stranded on a railway siding until it was collected for the next leg – and Port Lincoln (31 September).

The *Advertiser*, (24 September 1960) reported in a lead-up to the Port Lincoln visit that one of the members had described the IOG as 'a profit-sharing organisation that never makes a profit', and quoted Kathleen Steele Scott, when asked whether 'country people appreciated opera', as saying 'We've been playing to full houses. One Maitland woman said "They will talk about this for months" '. Some assistance was provided by local organisations, namely the Maitland Music Club and the Port Lincoln Players' Organisation who sponsored *A Dinner Engagement* with *The Telephone* and *The Scarf*, followed over two nights by *Susanna's Secret* with *Three's Company*. A review (*Advertiser*, 6 October) of the latter was generally favourable, but commented on the small audience. Undeterred, IOG found the adventure sufficiently rewarding to mount frequent country tours over the next twelve years.

Two years after IOG's large-scale *Albert Herring* came an even more ambitious undertaking – the Australian première of Britten's *The Turn of the Screw* based on Henry James's short story, only six years after its opening season at Teatro La Fenice, Venice. Joan Gill, Jacqueline Talbot, Janice Hearne and John Worthley were the brave singers who took on the leading roles – especially demanding given their comparative lack of experience with twentieth-century music – of the Governess, Miss Jessel, the Housekeeper and Peter Quint plus the Narrator. John Edmund, an English actor who had settled in Adelaide, was the director, Thomas Matthews, Leader and Deputy Conductor of the South Australian Symphony Orchestra, conducted the thirteen-piece chamber orchestra of players drawn from the SASO and Stan Ostoja-Kotkowski designed the sets for the Union Hall. Costing more than £1,700, this was a huge and extremely daring enterprise for what was basically an amateur company.

Through the good offices of Elder Professor John Bishop, a grant of £2,000 was secured from the Australian Elizabethan Theatre Trust to pay for the orchestra. But the audiences were embarrassingly small, and the IOG was left with a daunting (for those days) deficit of £800. A flurry of fund-raising events

Program cover design by Stan Ostoja-Kotkowski, *The Turn of the Screw*, 1960

including Tupperware parties and curry lunches was organised, but debts still outstanding after two years had to be written off.

John Horner wrote a serious and thoughtful review (*Advertiser*, 18 October 1960), criticising the clarity and strength of the singing, and suggesting obliquely that the work was vocally beyond the capacities of the cast. James Govenlock (*Sunday Mail*, 22 October 1960) was more tolerant, commending IOG for giving the Australian première of the work and for showing 'that Adelaide has a group of enthusiasts who can produce this form of entertainment with considerable skill'. Both writers praised the sets of Stan Ostoja-Kotkowski and the playing of the orchestra under Thomas Matthews. Some who saw it still recall their excitement at seeing and hearing this chilling account of lost innocence being produced by a local company.

(The author has vivid memories of this event. Her husband, Jim Silsbury, an agronomist with a passion for theatre and a great love of music, was Stage Director for the production. He was present through all the stage rehearsals and every performance, and she saw several of the six performances. Her recollections are of an extraordinarily forceful piece of music theatre, performed with conviction, although some of the voices were rather underpowered for the roles. She also remembers that the audiences were very small, but somehow it didn't seem to matter. At that time she had no involvement with, or responsibility for, the company's operations.)

In late 1960 John Worthley left Adelaide for the wider opportunities available in London, and soon secured a position with the professional choir of Westminster Cathedral. Elder Conservatorium singing teacher Barbara Howard, producer of many student and semi-professional operas, then became the musical figurehead for IOG. But it was Kathleen Steele Scott who attended to everything else – choosing repertoire and engaging casts and crews, organising city seasons, arranging trips to the country and visits to music clubs, making sure that halls were booked, that costumes and props were in their right places – doing all the odd jobs that nobody sees but which ensure that the show runs smoothly.

After the frenetic activity of 1960, and perhaps related to John Worthley's departure, IOG had a very quiet time in 1961. A single performance of *Three's Company*, with Neville Hicks replacing John Worthley, drew a full house to Stow Hall in August.

Robert Dawe, who went on to become known throughout the state and the country as a highly respected bass baritone (especially in oratorio), played his first role with IOG in a season during the 1962 Festival comprising *Gentleman's Island* written for the London-based Intimate Opera Company in 1958 by Joseph Horowitz (who had worked with it both as conductor and repetiteur), Poulenc's *La Voix Humaine* and *Prima Donna* by Australian composer Arthur Benjamin. Directors were Kathleen Steele Scott, Earl Bennett and Barbara Howard; Joan Sheard, Dorothy Oldham and Shirley Hicks were the conductor-pianists and Stan Ostojo-Kotkowski designed all three works.

In all, fifteen lunch-hour and evening performances were given at the Australia Hall in Angas Street – some of *Prima Donna* alone, others of the Poulenc and Horowitz and, in the evenings, all three. Again, one marvels at the stamina and dedication of the singers – each of the evening performances had been preceded by a midday show on the same day.

The season attracted two letters to the Editor of the *Sunday Mail*. One (17 March 1962 – 'Too Much', Norwood) claimed that 'Adelaide amateur groups are short-sighted in staging so many of their productions' during the Festival, and a reply (24 March, J. McEvoy, North Adelaide) defended the rights of the amateurs 'to display their talents (varied though they may be) to our visitors'.

John Horner (*Advertiser*, 21 March) reported on the season, commending especially Janice Hearne, who 'performed her memory feat perfectly and achieved continuous vocal beauty'. He was also prepared to give her 'the benefit of the theatrical doubt' in her efforts to strangle herself with a telephone cord while still singing. Of *Prima Donna* Mr Horner observed that 'Barbara Howard had a confident team who could all sing, act and be funny', and singled out Nancy Cullen for her 'perfect stage equilibrium'. His final paragraph reads: 'For 1964 this keen Intimate Opera Group deserves to be promoted from the "Fringe" and provided with a matching Intimate chamber orchestra.'

The program for the March 1962 season lists Kathleen Steele Scott as President, Jacqueline Talbot as Secretary, Joan Gill as Treasurer and Barbara Howard, William Harrison and Neville Hicks as other members of the Executive Committee. All functions continued to be carried out within the 'family'.

In August 1962 the Adelaide University Theatre Guild mounted a season comprising a play, a ballet and *Prima Donna*, using a number of the singers from the March production and directed by Hedley Cullen. IOG is not acknowledged in the program. Early in the following (non Festival) year IOG took *Gentleman's Island* and *Prima Donna* to the South Coast Festival at Victor Harbor, along with the company's sole excursion into conventional opera, a scene from Act I of *Madam* (sic) *Butterfly*, sung by Marie Bates and Malcolm Potter.

Between 1964 and 1970 IOG confined its productions mainly to the biennial Festivals, when full houses and balanced books could be expected, if not guaranteed. The reasons may well have been financial, but it is worth noting that during this period, and even going back to 1959, The Elder Conservatorium Opera Group was extremely active, largely due to baritone Arnold Matters, who had returned to his home town in 1959 after years of opera and oratorio experience in England and Europe and subsequently directed many operas for the Elder Conservatorium Opera Group. Starting with Smetana's *Two Widows* in July 1959, the ECOG presented fifteen seasons of operas and operatic excerpts during the following decade. Many of the Conservatorium students involved were regulars with IOG, and their availability might also have been a limiting factor.

During the 1964 Adelaide Festival of Arts, not yet in the official program but included among 'Other Events', IOG gave twelve lunch-hour and early evening performances in Mead Hall. *Three's Company* took the stage for the third time, with Janet Lasscock and Neville Hicks replacing two of the originals. Its composer Anthony Hopkins, who was in residence as Visiting Composer at the Elder Conservatorium for six months in 1964, attended the performances. Kathleen Steele Scott reported that he gave an introductory speech which was 'very interesting and amusing' and was 'quite taken aback to see an absolutely full house.' She remembered that returns from the box office for this season enabled IOG to pay off the last of their debts, and to accrue a small surplus of around £200.

Joan Gill, Ruth Gurner, Taverner Miller and Powell Harrison were among singers joining the company for Donizetti's domestic comedy *The Night Bell*. Barbara Howard restaged *Three's Company*, and Arnold Matters, working for the first time with IOG, directed the Donizetti. Shirley Hicks, Mary Painter (Handley) and Julian Mincham conducted the operas from the piano, and both operas were designed by Alexander McLeay. Harold Tidemann, ever a faithful admirer of the Group, still managed to find new ways of complimenting the company on the seventh repeat of its first production, and noted that the Donizetti, which 'attracted a capacity audience ... should prove a happy addition to the Intimate Opera Group's repertoire'. The program records that two more singers were added to the committee: Malcolm Potter to the Executive Committee, and May Cottle to the position of Secretary.

Having been so impressed by their production of *Three's Company*, Anthony Hopkins persuaded IOG to mount the Australian première of his new piece, *Hands Across the Sky*. The result was an ambitious Three Arts Program which played in the Arts Theatre in November for five nights. It opened with an unusual choice, Mozart's early piece *Bastien and Bastienne*, for which Mary Handley was the pianist, and tenor Anthony Neck and baritone Dean Patterson made their first of many appearances with the company. The Dalman Modern Ballet School – precursor of Australian Dance Theatre which was founded the following year, then presented six short ballets, all choreographed by Elizabeth Dalman or her mentor Eleo Pomare: *Smiles and Tears*, *The Girl With the Flaxen Hair*, *Giant Steps*, *Feline Fancies*, *Blues* and *Image*. Finally came the Hopkins piece, decribed in the program as 'After the original production by Anthony Hopkins'. It was sung by Powell Harrison, Marie Bates and Neville Hicks and accompanied by Shirley Hicks.

Kathleen Steele Scott was quite scathing about *Hands Across the Sky*, which she described as 'very silly ... Nothing like as clever as *Three's Company*'. The asperity of her reaction might have been coloured by the fact that IOG's good houses in the 1966 AFA enabled the company to pay off all their debts from preceding seasons, but then 'We lost the lot' on Hopkins. Her cashbook records expenditure of £10/2/6 on the event. However, long-standing ally Harold Tidemann (*Advertiser*, 4 November) was again favourably impressed with the satire on space research, concluding that 'the opera was altogether a brilliant success'.

During the 1966 Festival Yvonne Johnson, Max Pearce and Thomas Edmonds were among those who made their debuts with IOG in *Master Peters' Puppet Show* by de Falla, *If the Cap Fits* (another commission from IOC) by Geoffrey Bush and a return season of Wolf-Ferrari's comedy *Susanna's Secret*. Students of Western Teachers' College, where co-producer (with Barbara

Howard) Patricia Holmes lectured in music education, constructed Master Peter's puppets and designed all three works, and Anne Adamek and Judith Rodger were recruited as pianist-conductors.

Between 1964 and 1970 Intimate Opera put on eight separate seasons of mostly modern pieces, mostly self-funded, mainly one-acters, performed with piano accompaniment in small halls like the AMP Theatre and Mead Hall. *Three's Company*, Ravel's *L'Heure Espagnole*, Menotti's *The Telephone* and *The Old Maid and the Thief*, Arthur Benjamin's *Prima Donna*, Wolf-Ferrari's *Susanna's Secret* and others of the same ilk were shown around the city and on country tours.

Of special interest in IOG's program for the 1968 Adelaide Festival of Arts was *The Missus*, a commission based on the novel *We of the Never-Never* by Mrs Aeneas Gunn, from local composer David Gallasch and librettist Ruth Barratt. Polish designer Stan Ostoja-Kotkowski drew his first gum trees for the realistic set. John Horner (*Advertiser*, 12 March) commended the composer for making the music 'simply plain, stark, clumsy and outback like the men', and hailed the production as 'quite a feat, and quite a success'. Over a total of twenty lunch-hour and early evening performances, the Australian piece alternated with *Chanticleer* by Seymour Barab, an adaptation of Chaucer's Canterbury Tale of the fox and the cock, which was so popular during the Festival that a return season was mounted in the following September. Marie Bates and Janet Lasscock played the two women in *Chanticleer*; Dean Patterson was the fox and Thomas Edmonds the cock. John Horner called him 'the great scarlet Chanticleer – much given to self-admiration but remarkably quick to collapse at the slightest danger'.

Both men found themselves in the same position as the Adelaide Singers, who had raced from the their day jobs to opera engagements and back ten years earlier. To combine work at the Weapons Research Establishment at Salisbury, north of Adelaide, and opera in town, Dean Patterson used to add an hour's leave to his lunch break, ride his BMW motorbike the thirty kilometres into town, sing his role in Mead Hall and then return to his research at Salisbury. And Thomas Edmonds has reported 'My experience was similar (except that I drove a Morris Minor) viz., leave the classroom at Westminster School, belt into the city, make-up, dress, perform and belt back to school with runny black mascara rings around the eyes. Temperatures were usually in the mid-thirties. Forget lunch that day.'

Many of Adelaide's most respected musicians and theatre people were involved during this period: directors Barbara Howard, Arnold Matters, Hedley Cullen; pianists Alison Holder, Shirley Sawtell, Dorothy Oldham, Mary Handley, Margaret Lambert; singers Joan Gill, Leslie Dutton, Neville Hicks, Noel Robbins, Marie Bates, Malcolm Potter, Dean Patterson, Rae Cocking, Janice Hearne (now Chapman), Thomas Edmonds, Guila Tiver, Genty Stevens, Anthony Neck, Robert Dawe. Many of the singers went on to professional careers of considerable distinction, some continuing to work for the companies that succeeded IOG, some gaining national and international recognition.

In June 1969 IOG played *The Telephone* and *Three's Company* in the Matthew Flinders Theatre at Flinders University. Justin Macdonnell, at that time Lecturer in Drama at the University, recalls that this season came about through an invitation from the Flinders Music Advisory Committee to the company to present one of their series of lunch-hour concerts, and the offer expanded into two night-time shows. With hindsight, this event takes on greater importance than was evident at the time, as it marked the beginning of a long and fruitful co-operation between the company and the University.

IOG's persistence was at last rewarded, and its achievements recognised, through an official engagement by the 1970 Adelaide Festival of Arts to present Ravel's *L'Heure Espagnole* and Menotti's *The Old Maid and the Thief.* An advance grant from the Australian Elizabethan Theatre Trust promised financial security and enabled IOG to engage the noted Viennese-born, Sydney-resident director Stephan Beinl, an important step forward for an organisation which up to then had relied almost entirely on local talent, and a significant move towards professionalism. Sadly, Stephan Beinl died suddenly on the very eve of his departure for Adelaide. He was replaced by Stefan Haag, also originally from Vienna, who had established a highly respected national reputation for his opera productions, notably Menotti's *The Consul* for Australian National Theatre Movement in the early 1950s. His high standards ensured that IOG's houses were packed for nine lunch-hour and five night-time performances.

Kathleen Steele Scott and other IOG members recalled with obvious joy that the queue for admission reached from the AMP building on North Terrace 'right down and around into Hindley Street', and ascribed this popularity, at least in part, to the fact that Thomas Edmonds, who had recently won a national talent quest on television, played a major role. Kay Gallant substantiated this view with her story from the box office. She had told Tom about the 'ladies queueing up for hours to get a seat to see Thomas Edmonds – to hear Thomas Edmonds . . . and he wouldn't believe me. So I persuaded him to come into the box office, and I put him in a corner and covered him up with cartons, and I encouraged these ladies to ask their questions which consisted of "Is Thomas in this one?" And if I'd say "No", they'd go away and come back next day when he was. Anyhow he was there behind the boxes laughing hysterically. I could see the boxes shaking.'

This season received a grant from the Special Projects Fund of the Australian Council for the Arts, and, to the amazement of IOG, actually made a profit. No, they were told by their benefactor, you can't give it back. Use it for something else. Local theatre director Chris Winzar put it to good use by running classes in stage technique and acting followed by a workshop season of scenes from *Pagliacci* and *Hansel and Gretel*, and on 25 and 26 October Bartok's *Bluebeard's Castle* (complete) at Theatre 62. Always supportive, Harold Tidemann (*Advertiser*, 26 October) commended IOG for 'going all experimental', singling out Dean Patterson for his 'convincing performance as the hypnotic Bluebeard' and Mary Handley for her 'playing of the fascinating music' in Bartok's one-acter.

Kay Gallant and Mary Handley have reported that, from the 1970 Festival season onwards, there were 'mutterings' backstage and at cast parties about the possibility of a professional opera company being formed in South Australia. In 1968 the government had announced plans to build a Festival Theatre on the banks of the River Torrens. The gossip was that Don Dunstan, who became Premier on 30 May 1970 and subsequently assumed personal responsibility for the arts, was interested in the formation of an opera company which could perform in the new theatre. The secretary's records show that everyone involved in the 1970 Festival of Arts season had been paid $15 – hardly a fortune, but a significant amount for people who had become accustomed to using their own money for the privilege of putting on operas, and enough to make them more than mildly interested in the prospect of earning money from performing as well as fulfilling their ambitions.

Despite the success of the Ravel-Menotti season, IOG mounted no further fully staged productions in 1970 or 1971. It seems likely that, having tasted the benefits of government funding – which enabled the Group to engage professional directors, to pay all their casts and crews and to emerge from a demanding season with no deficit and enhanced reputations – the old days of shoestrings and oily rags, of begging, borrowing and making do and relying on everybody's generosity and goodwill, had quite suddenly lost their charm. And the rumours that a fully professional company was in the offing were powerful incentives to look more closely at their standards. There was a spotlight lurking. With luck it might fall on them, and they had to be ready.

They did not have to wait long.

3

Fortunately

Four's a Crowd – 1972

*T*he whole world of Intimate Opera changed dramatically and irrevocably in 1972.

During the Adelaide Festival of Arts that March, IOG played a triple bill of *The Wandering Scholar* (Gustav Holst), *The Glittering Gate* (Peggy Glanville-Hicks) and Pergolesi's *La Serva Padrona* in the AMP Theatre on the corner of North Terrace and King William Street. A grant was secured from the Australian Council for the Arts to assist with production costs.

The program for this season names Kathleen Steele Scott as IOG's President, Dean Patterson as Vice-President, Kay Gallant as Secretary, Joy Williamson as Treasurer and Mary Handley, Laura Harrison, Barbara Howard and Elizabeth Wood as Committee members.

Between Tuesday 14 and Saturday 25 March, IOG mounted 18 lunch-hour performances of single operas and presented all three on five nights.

John Milson, co-founder (with Richard Divall) of Young Opera, Sydney, came from Perth to direct the triple bill and Ross Anderson was his designer. Malcolm John accompanied *La Serva Padrona* with Michel Brunsden (violin) and Judith Luck (cello), and Mary Handley played for *The Wandering Scholar* and *The Glittering Gate*, the latter with Michael Holland (percussion). The addition of these orchestral instruments was a major step for IOG,

Daphne Harris and Dean Patterson,
The Wandering Scholar, 1972

made possible because of the ACA grant. Strong casts were assembled – Robert Dawe, Janet Lasscock and Michael Lewis as the mute (Mary Handley remembers thinking at the time that this was a criminal waste of a wonderful voice) for Pergolesi, Dean Patterson, Daphne Harris, William Harrison and Anthony Clark for Holst, and Anthony Clark and Michael Lewis for Glanville-Hicks.

During the lead-up to the 1972 Festival, IOG committee member Elizabeth Wood, then a musicology student at the Elder Conservatorium with a special interest in opera by Australian composers, had the clever notion of publicising *The Wandering Scholar* by holding a rehearsal on the Festival Theatre's foundations during the building workers' lunch break. VIPs, including the Premier, agreed to attend. A witty story in the *News* revealed that the plan was nearly stymied by the Adelaide City Council, on the grounds that any injuries caused to guests would not be covered by compensation. The unnamed journalist reported gleefully 'The show would most certainly not go on, sang officialdom from the Town Hall'. IOG took legal advice and found that they could not be stopped as long as they only played to the workers. So the VIPs missed out, but the show did go on.

All the performers had to wear hard hats, and Mary Handley recalls that her piano was lifted in by a crane that loomed over her while she played. When Daphne Harris, playing the would-be-wandering wife Alison, swung her pearls in a flirtatious gesture, they flew off over her head and landed in a deep pit behind her, where they remain to this day. IOG members still like to claim that their traditions are built into the theatre's very foundations, and that they were the first company to perform there. The photograph of this history-making event is still prized.

Of the three operas, Harold Tidemann clearly preferred *The Wandering Scholar*, writing (*Advertiser*, 15 March) that Dean Patterson and Daphne Harris sang and acted 'with perfect ease' and director John Milson 'achieved splendid results'.

Considering that Adelaide is a small city – less than a million at that time – it is interesting to note that IOG survived, and from time to time flourished, quite independently of the academic music institutions, especially the major one, the Elder Conservatorium at the University of Adelaide.

Of their own accord, however, staff from the Elder had been involved in productions from the beginning. It was singing teacher Max Worthley who first suggested to his brother John that he should form his own company. Barbara Howard, also a member of the vocal staff, directed IOG's first production (and many others thereafter) and held committee positions with the company. Her colleague Arnold Matters followed her example for three operas in the 1960s. Alison Holder, also a member of staff, played for a number of productions and J.V. Peters was the conductor for *Albert Herring* in 1958. Elder Professor John Bishop acted as 'angel' for the company when he secured a grant, the company's first, for *The Turn of the Screw* in 1960. In addition, many IOG singers were students at the Conservatorium, and their names appear in many of the cast lists of both organisations. Anthony Hopkins, composer of the original *Three's Company* – and, incidentally, instrumental in both the formation and the naming of the company – was Visiting Composer at the Elder Conservatorium in 1964. Not only did he attend his own opera during the Adelaide Festival of Arts but he was also the impetus for IOG to mount his *Hands Across the Sky* later that year. Patricia Holmes, lecturer in music at Western Teachers' College, was co-producer with Barbara Howard of *Master Peter's Puppet Show* in the 1964 Adelaide Festival of Arts.

Connections with the state's second university, Flinders University of SA, were initiated in 1969.

Justin Macdonnell, then a Lecturer in Drama at Flinders University, had been involved in the 1969 engagement, and continued to follow the IOG because of his interest in twentieth-century music and opera. Of the 1972 season, knowing of the 'mutterings', he has recalled thinking that 'It could be the basis of something quite exciting'.

Any performance of music by Australian composers was bound to attract the attention of Sydney musician James Murdoch. He had returned to Australia in 1972, after four years of managing and entrepreneuring in England and Europe, (including being the founding director of Peter Maxwell Davies's contemporary music group The Pierrot Players (later The Fires of London)) as music consultant to the Australian Council for the Arts, especially on the promotion of Australian composers and their music. As his particular passion was – and still is – Peggy Glanville-Hicks, he was of course in Adelaide to see her opera, and to report on the Festival's Australian content.

Meanwhile, musicologist Professor Andrew McCredie at the University of Adelaide and Dene Barnett, Lecturer in Philosophy at the Flinders University of South Australia, had developed a research project into a production for the same Festival. At the Bonython Hall, down the road from the AMP Theatre, Rameau's *Pygmalion* endeavoured to reproduce, in every authentic detail, the performance practices of a production of the opera at Fontainebleau in 1754, including fresh flowers on the women's gowns for each performance, and illumination by candle light. Into the small world of opera in South Australia it brought Justin Macdonnell as Administrator and Stage Director, and myself, lecturer in music at the adjoining Bedford Park Teachers' College, as repetiteur and continuo player. My especially delicate harpsichord, crafted by the distinguished German maker Martin Skowronek, was owned by Dene Barnett, who personally honed the plectra from authentic goosequill. Barnett, one of the country's earliest scholars to proselytise for greater authenticity in the performance of seventeenth- and eighteenth-century opera, had had his attention drawn to Richard Divall, who had already established a fine reputation as an exponent of baroque music in Sydney. Divall was therefore the natural choice for conductor of this ambitious (and not entirely successful) project.

Noted Sydney soprano Marilyn Richardson made her Adelaide debut, alternating with Margaret MacPherson in the role of L'Amour and with Gaye MacFarlane (also from Sydney) for the opening cantata *The Forges of Lemnos* by Nicolas Bernier. Gaye MacFarlane sang Cephise, Sheila McCarthy was the Statue and Malcolm Potter played Pygmalion. Dene Barnett produced the event and Ton Witsel, a teacher and performer of mime then on the staff of Flinders University, was the director. In the chorus were the Corinthian Singers, some of whose members caught the opera virus and sang in many subsequent productions.

There were hazards attendant on authenticity. One night during the performance Malcolm Potter, as Pygmalion, was extolling in song the glories of the fires of love when a bunch of candles detached itself from the chandelier above. Had he not unwittingly stepped aside at the crucial moment his head, as well as his heart, would have caught fire.

For many in the audience, peering through the candle-lit gloom, however authentic, gave them little more than a vague notion of the action, but Harold Tidemann (*Advertiser*, 18 March) described the French opera-ballet as 'sheer delight'. He found that the 'singer-actors aquitted themselves with distinction', the dancers 'made an enchanting spectacle', 'the designer Pamela MacFarlane cannot be too highly praised and the mime and choreography by Ton Witsel was meticulous'. He observed that 'The Conductor, Richard Divall, was in perfect control of the musicians who gave a faithful interpretation of the score'. He even admired the work of the repetiteur. She incidentally, spent the entire season in a state of high anxiety, fearing that one of the delicate quills would lose its point and leave her with no B flat. It happened in rehearsal, but fortunately not in performance.

As well as promoting home-grown music, James Murdoch had been charged by the Australian Council for the Arts with sussing out individuals and organisations that might be eligible for subsidy under the policies already on the drawing board, including the establishment of a virtually new national organisation to fund and promote the arts, for implementation in the (likely) event of a Labor win in the forthcoming 1972 Federal election. He initiated discussions with Kathleen Steele Scott, aiming to determine whether IOG had any interest in forming the nucleus of a publicly funded state opera company. It certainly had.

This interest came into confluence with that of the state government of SA. Don Dunstan's accession to the premiership in 1970 began what is still referred to as the 'Dunstan Decade'. As Premier he brought about a revolution in government support for the arts, taking upon himself the relevant responsibilities. He recounts in *Felicia, The Political Memoirs of Don Dunstan* that in November 1970 he engaged (poached, to be blunt) 'Len Amadio, then local Concert Manager for the Australian Broadcasting Commission', creating for him a special position within the Premier's Department with 'briefs for work in both the arts and tourist development'. Very soon Amadio was totally absorbed by his work for the arts, and a 'small Arts Development Branch of the Department was set up, which he headed'.

In *The Dunstan Decade* Andrew Parkin and Allan Patience spell out the detail. Len Amadio was appointed Development Officer for the Arts and Tourism in November 1970 and became a member of the Policy Secretariat in the Premier's Department. In September 1973 a separate Arts Development Branch was formed, to be upgraded in 1977 to Arts Development Division with Len Amadio as Director, a position he held with considerable distinction until 1991, when bureaucratic changes revised his status to Senior Adviser in the Department of Arts and Cultural Heritage. He resigned in 1995.

By 1972 South Australia already had its own companies for theatre (The State Theatre Company 1975) and contemporary dance (Australian Dance Theatre 1965), and wanted an opera company to complete the trilogy. And, of course, to catch up with the other states – by this time regional opera companies had been established in New South Wales, Victoria and Western Australia.

Many meetings to discuss the establishment of a state-funded opera company were held in Adelaide and Sydney (at the Australian Council for the Arts) over the following months. Representatives of IOG and Flinders University, Len Amadio, James Murdoch (when he was in town) and occasionally Richard Divall (from 24 May Musical Director of Victoria State Opera) gathered under the chairmanship of Kathleen Steele Scott, who ensured a general spirit of enthusiastic co-operation. The burning question was whether any new company should build on IOG, or start all over from scratch.

As part of the search for an answer, less than four months after its marathon season in the 1972 Festival, Intimate Opera accepted a second invitation from the Flinders Music Advisory Committee (FMAC) to perform in the Matthew Flinders Theatre. In the files for this event is a General Statement of Intention, attached to the application to the Australian Council for the Arts (ACA) for a guarantee against loss of $2,636 for the season comprising Handel's *Overture to Xerxes*, a dramatised version of *Agrippina*, also by Handel, and *The Night Bell* by Donizetti.

The Statement acknowledges that the Group must 'mount a season outside the umbrella of the Festival organisation' and admits to 'deficiencies . . . in the technical area, administration and promotion'. The assistance of Flinders University with production services is acknowledged, as is the offer from the Adelaide Festival of Arts to allow their Publicity Manager, Doug Loan, to act as consultant. The file also notes that The South Australian Theatre Company had agreed to make its Wardrobe Master, Laurence Blake, available to assist with costumes. This level of collaboration and co-operation between different arts bodies in Adelaide was unprecedented, and indicates not only general interest from the established organisations in the fledgling, but also their willingness to help it learn to fly.

Putting on operas in a fully equipped professional theatre with an orchestra, largely comprising students and staff from the Elder Conservatorium, a chorus, a professional conductor (Richard Divall) and professional designers and directors was a monumental change for a company accustomed to church halls and institutes, piano accompaniments, small casts of soloists, no conductor apart from the pianists, and costumes out of the singers' wardrobes. Justin Macdonnell was the main driver. Kathleen Steele Scott observed in her *Oral History* that in 1972 'Justin was doing it all. I wasn't.' Maybe not, but her presence was strongly felt all the same.

The production team included staff members of Flinders University – Justin Macdonnell (Administration), Murray Copland (Director and translator for Agrippina) and Quentin Hole (sets for both operas). I played continuo for Handel and trained the Donizetti chorus. And although his name does not appear among the program credits, Russell Mitchell recalls that his interest in and flair for opera administration began as a Flinders drama student working backstage on *Agrippina*. He is now Business Affairs Director at Opera Australia.

Because of widespread discussion of the possibility that a permanent company might be formed, the Flinders season attracted considerable advance publicity. Helen Covernton (*Advertiser*, 1 July) wrote 'With these two new productions the Intimate Opera Group could enter a new stage of development and become the state's acknowledged Regional Opera Company'. Liz Blieschke (*Advertiser*, 8 July) was even more direct. 'When the Intimate Opera Group performs at the Flinders University next week, it will be an ambitious attempt to seek recognition as SA's regional opera company.' In the same article, Dean Patterson, director for *The Night Bell* and Vice President of IOG, is quoted as saying that the time was right for SA to establish its own opera company, expressing the hope that agreement could be reached by 'all the interested opera people in SA'. The report included the expectation of IOG President Kathleen Steele Scott that the formation of an administration for the new professional group would be finalised by December 1972.

In the program for the operas at Flinders University she wrote: 'We believe that tonight's performance, in which we are proud to be associated with the Flinders University, is a significant step towards securing a flourishing future for opera in South Australia with a permanent professional company.'

The 'mutterings and mumblings' had at last found public expression, and not just in SA. During the planning stages of the Flinders season Justin Macdonnell wrote to Sydney music critic Maria Prerauer thanking her for publicising the event in the *Sunday Australian* and the *Daily Telegraph*. His PS reads: 'All the rumours you were supposed not to have heard about Intimate Opera's intended bid for status as South Australia's regional opera are quite correct.'

The Flinders season was well attended and favourably reviewed. Ralph Middenway (*Advertiser*, 15 July 1972) wrote 'Last night the Intimate Opera and Michael Lewis came of age. This was far and away the best night we've had from this group, upon whom so many of us have publicly pinned our hopes for a real professional opera company in this state'. Referring specifically to the Donizetti, he commended the design, the direction and the music for sharing 'a flair and a saucy distinction', found that 'the total performance was musically and dramatically balanced', and commended Michael Lewis for his 'spectacularly funny role as Enrico'. The critic was less enthusiastic about *Agrippina*, finding the 'conjunction of styles uneasy', but was impressed by the 'emotional intensity' with which Genty Stevens sustained the 'cruelly difficult' role.

From July onwards, IOG was extremely busy on two fronts. Many formal and informal meetings were held dealing with the complexities of transforming amateur into professional status. In between, old and new commitments to performing engagements had to be fulfilled.

The Flinders University season ended on 16 July. A mere three days later the IOG committee met and agreed that Justin Macdonnell and I should be invited to join their deliberations.

Less than a week later, on 23 July, a second meeting set up a Steering Committee comprising IOG faithfuls Kay Gallant, Mary Handley, Laura Harrison, Barbara Howard, Dean Patterson, Elizabeth Wood and of course Kathleen Steele Scott; from Flinders University Justin Macdonnell, myself and Vernon Lewis, a student who had shown a considerable flair for music administration; and from the University of Adelaide Ralph Middenway and Grahame Dudley. Lawyer Brian Hunter, a friend of Kathleen's known to be an opera enthusiast, took the chair.

Next on the Group's timetable was the most extensive touring schedule of its whole existence, almost as though singing a swansong to its old life, and weighty matters of re-organisation had to be set aside for most of August while IOG took a double bill of standards, *Prima Donna* and *Susanna's Secret*, to five towns in the Mid-North and Eyre Peninsula from 21–26 August, and in eight more in the Upper Murray and Southeast from 21–28 August.

Another radical departure was in store. At a meeting on 24 August sandwiched in between touring it was reported that James Murdoch had approached IOG with an offer of $4,000 from the Council for Assistance to Australian Composers to celebrate the 75th birthday of the composer Margaret Sutherland. Her only opera, *The Young Kabbarli*, had had its première in Hobart on 19 August 1965 at a conference dealing with operas by Australian composers, and James Murdoch was determined to honour a woman he had always held in very high esteem. Having failed to persuade other companies to take on the sensitive task of mounting an opera about the eccentric Daisy Bates and her interventions on behalf of Aborigines on a remote Catholic mission at Beagle Bay in outback Western Australia, he turned to SA, hoping that IOG's aspirations would assist his cause. As he rightly judged, IOG was in the mood for adventures, and his offer was accepted.

On 18 October the Steering Committee met and considered a draft

Janet Lasscock, Wendy McMurtrie, Alan Crooks, William Harrison, Daphne Harris
and Dean Patterson, *Prima Donna* Country Tour, 1972

constitution. It was agreed that a Special General Meeting be held on Monday 4 December, the agenda to include adoption of the constitution and the election of President, Treasurer, Board of Management and Artistic Committee. A sub-committee comprising Brian Hunter, Ralph Middenway, Elizabeth Wood and myself, with Kathleen Steele Scott as a proxy, was delegated to 'determine and implement' the positions of Administrator and Secretary, and to reach their decisions by no later than 15 December. This sub-committee received a suggestion that the selection committee they would propose should include at least one person from outside IOG. These matters required detailed thought and planning, because the two main positions under question would be paid, a new and, to most members, strange state of affairs to be approached with considerable caution.

At a subsequent meeting on 31 October more names were suggested for the Board and it was agreed that the Interim Artistic Committee should meet to

William Harrison and Daphne Harris, *Prima Donna* Country Tour, 1972

'assess the suggested February program'. In the absence of formal minutes on this point, the best guess of several of those involved is that Justin Macdonnell, anticipating his appointment as Administrator, had already drawn up plans for the new company's first season.

Meanwhile, *Kabbarli* rehearsals began in the music room of Bedford Park Teachers' College. (Smudges from the powder used to blacken the exposed skin of the fake Aborigines remained on the walls for many years.) Because *Kabbarli* was a short piece of only one act, a program comprising the opera, preceded by brackets of Sutherland songs from baritones John McKenzie and Dean Patterson, Carol Kohler (soprano), Norma Hunter (mezzo soprano) and Alan Bray (clarinet) was compiled. Performances were held in The Olde King's Music Hall in Adelaide on 13 and 14 November and as part of a week-long birthday celebration on 29 and 30 November in the Great Hall of the National Gallery of Victoria in Melbourne.

The *Young Kabbarli* libretto, based on an incident in the life of Daisy Bates, was written by Maie Casey, and is frankly over-sentimental and dated in its language and plot. ('O list to the sound of the didgeridu [*sic*]', sings the dewey-eyed Kabbarli.) Most of the characters are Aborigines, and were sung by whites in blackface. Dean Patterson was the rebellious Goonderwell whose antics provided the gist of the story, Carol Kohler, Jennifer Hope and Norma Hunter from the Adelaide Singers were the Aboriginal girls, John McKenzie was the Trappist brother and Genty Stevens played Kabbarli, the Aboriginal name for grandmother given to Daisy Bates.

The cast included dancer David Gulpilil and didjeridu player Dick Bundilil, both full-blood Aborigines. Lecturer in dance at Flinders Moshe Kedem directed, the design was by Richard Sobczak and Patrick Thomas conducted the ten-piece orchestra. Justin Macdonnell managed administration and promotions, and the names of IOG regulars Kay Gallant, Mary Handley and Laura Harrison are listed under backstage credits.

Sketch by Charles Blackman for the facsimile score of *The Young Kabbarli*, 1972

As I remember from my perspective as repetiteur and pianist, no concern was felt over the political and social appropriateness of the event at the time. In retrospect there was considerable cause for embarrassment, but the dramatic and musical demands of the piece fully occupied the energies of cast, orchestra and crew, leaving no room for questions of propriety. Sharing the stage with two Aborigines was a complete novelty for the performers, and in some measure at least gave the production authenticity.

In keeping with the celebratory nature of the occasion, sherry was served from 7.30 and the $6.00 ticket price included supper.

Harold Tidemann (*Advertiser*, 14 November) declared the event a 'definite contribution to the performing arts', describing the piece as a 'remarkable fusion of old and new'. His summary runs: 'The intrusion of Daisy Bates and the Church on native legends, superstitions and beliefs was vividly illustrated in both the music and the action.'

The audiences responded favourably, especially to the dancing and playing of the two Aborigines. There were some reservations. At supper after the première, the Premier, Don Dunstan, whose encouragement of the whole project had been crucial, said 'I was not expecting *The Ring*, but this is not quite what I had in mind either'. It seemed appropriate that he was standing with his back to a corner at the time.

More than two decades later, I told him about my history of SOSA and asked if he remembered his reaction to *Kabbarli*. He certainly did. When I quoted the above to him, he laughed and said that he did not recall the exact words, but would not object if I reported him thus.

1972 was probably the last time that *The Young Kabbarli* could have been performed. By March 1973 the Australia Council had been formed. Its boards included one for Aboriginal Arts. The time for paying less than full respect to indigenous culture was definitely over and the days of blackface, in Australia at least, were gone forever.

Although the drama of Margaret Sutherland's opera must be confined to its own time, her music is admirable in its capacity to create an atmosphere that sets indigenous and European musical practices and idioms side by side while preserving the integrity of both. Early in 1973 Patrick Thomas conducted a recording of the whole work – the first quadraphonic LP of an Australian opera.

The status of the event is reflected in the Melbourne program, which was graced by commendations from R.J. Hamer, Premier of Victoria, H.C. Coombs, Chairman Australian Council for the Arts, and Eric Westbrook, Director, National Gallery of Victoria. The program for the Adelaide season carried a foreword by Kathleen Steele Scott stating IOG's aim to 'establish a fully professional regional opera company in South Australia'.

The Young Kabbarli was the last production of the Intimate Opera Group.

4

Interlude

❧

The Young Kabbarli may have been the final production of Intimate Opera Group, but for many of the people who had guided this extraordinary organisation for 25 years it was merely the closing of one chapter and the opening of another. Or perhaps the end of the introduction and the beginning of the main story. Their names are dotted through the IOG annals as performers, committee members, backstage workers and organisers, and will re-appear bearing various offices and fulfilling a range of roles in the following chapters. Some continued to work for the companies that replaced IOG, others moved on into other opera and theatre companies, captured inescapably in their impressionable years by the lure of opera.

This continuity is a matter for some wonderment. In many other cities in Australia, and probably around the world, professional opera companies have been formed at the expense of amateur ones, causing a deal of bitterness and resentment among those who felt that they had not been properly appreciated and rewarded. It simply did not happen in South Australia. The main reason was that the Group's president, Kathleen Steele Scott, embraced the change, putting the interests of opera ahead of her own personal ambitions, and her

IOG team, accustomed as they were to trusting her in all matters (including, in many cases, their private lives) followed her lead. I was closely involved in the discussions preceding the decision to go ahead with the new arrangements, and cannot recall a single occasion when there was any serious difference of opinion.

In all the dealings there is no doubt that the presence of Kathleen Steele Scott was crucial. Where there could have been noses out of joint and bitterness at what might have appeared as a takeover by operatic *nouveaux riches*, there was never anything but gratitude and excitement that the years of struggle were at last paying off, and that the state was to have a properly recognised opera company. At the centre of all the negotiations, providing the example of leadership and co-operation that had characterised all her years with IOG, was this remarkable woman, always ready to talk things over, expert at ensuring that tender egos were not too badly damaged, radiating enthusiasm and common sense.

Apart from her general good influence, the practices she had helped to instil at IOG continued to affect opera in South Australia for at least another twenty years.

As with the people, so with the principles. During its 25 years, IOG performed more than 20 operas written in the twentieth century, put on over 20 seasons and gave more than a hundred actual performances in Adelaide, Melbourne and country centres in the South East, Riverland, Mid North and Iron Triangle. The repertoire that got the company started back in 1957, and most of the pieces played by IOG up to 1972, were contemporary. The choice of recently written chamber works was determined partly by what was available, and by the limited resources they required, but taste for modern music theatre was also a major factor. Admittedly, many were one-acters with piano accompaniment, designed for performance in the modest surroundings of church halls and institutes rather than grand opera houses. Many of the pieces were minor, but they came from significant composers – Menotti, Wolf-Ferrari, de Falla, Ravel, Holst and Peggy Glanville-Hicks. Among them were *Albert Herring* (1958) and the Australian première of *The Turn of the Screw* (1960), both by Benjamin Britten and both distinctly major. As will be seen, the leaning towards contemporary operas flowed through into the new company that replaced

IOG in 1973. I believe that the traditions established by IOG and its successors exerted a strong influence on the choice of operas for the biennial Adelaide Festivals of Arts. South Australia's record for presenting major twentieth-century operas, some in their Australian premières, is unequalled in this country. Outstanding among them are *Troilus and Cressida* (1964), the three parable operas of Benjamin Britten (1972), *The Adventures of Mr Broucek* (1974), *Wozzeck* (1976), *The Midsummer Marriage* (1978), *Death in Venice* (1980), *The Makropulos Affair* (1982), *Lady Macbeth of Mtsensk* (1984), *Voss* (1986), *The Fiery Angel* (1988), *Nixon in China* (1992) and *Writing to Vermeer* (2000).

A tally carried out for the twentieth anniversary edition of Australia's national journal *Opera-Opera* counted more than 100 twentieth-century operas performed in South Australia over the period 1957–1997 (Elizabeth Silsbury, *Scorebook*, 1997).

The stated policy of New Opera South Australia, the company that succeeded IOG from 1973, was to avoid Grand Opera and to concentrate on new and old works. This policy proved unworkable and was modified after about three years, when more conventional repertoire became the standard fare.

But in the Adelaide Festivals, every even year from 1964 until 1992 and again in 2000, a major twentieth-century opera not previously seen in Australia attracted devotees from all over the country. It has always been my contention that this practice grew out of the groundwork of IOG.

5

From Amateur to Professional
in One Huge Leap – 1973

⚬

Once *Kabbarli*, a major enterprise for what was still essentially an amateur company, was over, things moved very quickly. Although there are no documents recording IOG's decision to transform itself into a fully professional organisation, the surviving key players of 1972 are in agreement that by mid November the change was virtually *fait accompli*. During November and December (as well as rehearsing and performing *Kabbarli* in Adelaide and Melbourne) matters had progressed to the point where advertisements could be placed locally and nationally for the position of administrator. A closing date of 18 November was given, and interviews were called for 28 November. A Special General Meeting on 4 December adopted both the constitution and the new name, New Opera, South Australia, chosen with no dissension as reflecting both the newness of the company and the originality (in Australia at least) of its policies.

A major factor in IOG's acceptance of the radical change in status was the recognition that, while many of their performances were musically and dramatically acceptable, they were seriously deficient in many aspects of their management. Choosing the right person as the new organisation's chief executive was essential.

From mid 1971, when arrangements were being put in place for a production of Rameau's *Pygmalion* for the 1972 Adelaide Festival of Arts under the guidance of its Director Louis van Eyssen, Justin Macdonnell's energy and passion for opera had been a vital element in the progress of a highly complicated operation, in which extreme sensitivities were often uncomfortably close to the surface. As administrator and stage director for *Pygmalion* he was unfailingly efficient and also managed to sustain, through his own enthusiasm for the intellectual values of the production, the flagging resources of actors and musicians who found the producer Dene Barnett unreasonable and often impossible to satisfy. His lack of sympathy for Sheila McCarthy, three months pregnant and frequently feeling faint and nauseated when directed to stand for long periods during rehearsals, was typical of his somewhat inhuman expectations of his cast, musicians and crew.

Throughout the rehearsals and performances of *Pygmalion* Macdonnell's ambition to become an opera manager crystallised. He says now that he never knew he wanted to run an opera company until he found himself doing it.

He was intimately involved through all IOG's productions and negotiations in late 1972 and early 1973, and his clearsightedness and common sense, not to mention his ability to work amicably with both the former IOG decision-makers and the newcomers, were important factors in easing the transition.

It would have been simpler, quicker and cheaper to appoint him directly to the senior administrative position, and some of those on the new authority were in favour of going ahead and handing him, on a plate, the position he had clearly earned. He says that by September 1972 he knew that he would run the new company, and pressure from Professor Wal Cherry of the Flinders University Drama Department about his intentions regarding his position as lecturer in 1973 merely helped to determine his ambitions. But there were other contenders – after all, this was Adelaide's first professional opera administration position ever – and now that government money was at stake public service protocols must be observed.

The job description ran as follows.

A new constitution has been drawn up to provide an appropriate structure for a regional opera company. There is to be a Board of Management comprising of six people who will be responsible for the legal and financial affairs of the company, and an Artistic Committee, also with a membership of six, who will make all decisions relating to the choice of operas and their production. A schools subcommittee is to work in conjunction with the Artistic Committee on presentation of opera to young audiences ... The Administrator will be responsible for implementing decisions made by the Board of Management and the Artistic Committee.

There were fourteen applicants, all from South Australia. Four were interviewed, and on 15 December 1972 Justin Macdonnell was duly appointed as the state's first professional opera administrator. An IOG meeting was held on 20 December – Christmas must have taken a back seat that year – attended by Grahame Dudley, Elizabeth Wood, Dean Patterson, Laura Harrison, Linda Bates, Justin Macdonnell and Kay Gallant, who was appointed Assistant Administrator/Secretary, and Linda Bates, who became Press Officer.

By the end of January 1973, the state government had pledged $15,000 and NOSA was incorporated. Its board, elected by members who had paid a small subscription fee, comprised engineer Richard Brown (Chairman), Kathleen Steele Scott, lawyer Brian Hunter, singer-scientist Dean Patterson and businessman, Ion Ullett. Kathleen Steele Scott, Dean Patterson and I were appointed to the Artistic Committee and Alan Farwell, Music Supervisor in the Education Department, Grahame Dudley, Lecturer in Music Education at the Elder Conservatorium and myself to the Schools' Committee.

An office for the Administrator (Justin Macdonnell) and Secretary (Kay Gallant) was set up at 55 Rowland Road, Hilton, directly opposite the small but lively Theatre 62, something of a change from Kappy's Coffee Lounge in the city, where they had hitherto conducted their business. Two more IOG veterans, Laura Harrison and Elizabeth Wood, were appointed Stage Director and Research Officer respectively. Linda Bates shared her position of Press Officer with Theatre 62. The list of Patrons was most impressive – Lady Bonython, a scion of the Adelaide establishment, Antony Hopkins, Barbara Howard, Arnold Matters and Margaret Sutherland, whose 75th birthday had been honoured by IOG in December 1972.

Agreement was quickly reached on an artistic policy for the new company.

Quite clearly, traditional grand opera was out; modern chamber – intimate, in fact – opera was in. New Opera issued a press release undertaking to 'continue Intimate Opera Group's commitment to works of the twentieth century performed in English' and to concentrate on 'works that are … dramatically viable as well as musically significant and on singers as actors'. Promises were made to take works 'devised or chosen especially for touring conditions to school and country centres', to employ local singers 'as often as possible' and 'to make a positive contribution to the growth of an Australian repertoire by providing young composers, especially South Australians, with an opportunity to test their work in a performance situation'.

These conclusions were reached via two routes. Firstly, the tastes of the staff, the board generally and the Artistic Committee leaned away from the standard grand operas and towards smaller pieces with greater emphasis on dramatic content and less on vocal display for its own sake. The policy-makers believed that a major change could be wrought in the art form by challenging singers to take as much trouble with their dramatic effectiveness as with their singing. They were well aware that most opera directors at the time were musicians, many of them singers, and often demanded little beyond musical competence from their casts. One of the ideals of the new policy was to revolutionise the way that opera was regarded, both by performers and audiences, and to develop a greater respect for the total, not just the musical, impact of the art form.

The policy allowed exploration of repertoire in contemporary music, in early music and in works by Australian composers, all fields of special interest to the organisers. Programs would aim to present both new and recent works and unjustly neglected pre-classical ones, as well as to promote what was expected to be a flowering of new home-grown pieces.

In fact, the style of Intimate Opera Group was to be perpetuated by a new intimate style of professional opera company.

Australian works were to be given especial attention. The Australian Council of the Arts had just been set up (in March 1973) by the newly-elected Labor Government. Seven boards were appointed, including one for music, with a strong commitment to provide financial assistance for Australian composers in the form of commissions and subsidies for performances. Opera was initially assigned to the Theatre Board, but at one of its first meetings the

Music Board moved to assume responsibility for an art form which was predominantly music, and the drama people put up no resistance. They were wiser than they knew at the time – opera has been the single biggest customer and the worst headache of all art forms within the Council's provenance from March 1973 until the present, and probably ever more shall be so. It's the nature of the beast.

The second reason for choosing to operate on a small scale, quite apart from the artistic and idealistic considerations, was to keep costs to a reasonable level, those responsible being mindful of how easily huge amounts of money can be consumed by large orchestras and choruses, and by the lavish sets and costumes on which many grand operas depend.

Press responses to the news were in the main enthusiastic. Helen Covernton (*Sunday Mail*, 2 February 1973) wrote: 'If New Opera South Australia can produce interesting and entertaining opera, it will be marvellous', and warned that the company 'will need an open mind, a sense of fun and the ability to take criticism'. Greg Kelton (*Advertiser*, 28 March 1973) reported: 'SA now has its own fully professional opera company. But don't expect opera with Viking ladies clad in breast-plates and horned helmets, singing of unrequited love – in Italian'. An accompanying photograph shows the Administrator

John Greene, Lucelle Taylor, Eric Maddison and Belinda Matonti with Justin Macdonnell

with four singers intended as the nucleus of the company – sopranos Lucelle Taylor and Belinda Matonti, tenor Eric Maddison and baritone John Greene were engaged on full-time contracts to carry out the schools program and perform in city seasons.

By the end of February a brochure was released announcing plans for an ambitious program of three city seasons plus extensive schools and country touring. Apart from the eagerness of the administrator, the board and the various committees to get a show on the road, there was pressing urgency on the political front as well.

On the banks of the River Torrens, Adelaide's first government-funded theatre was nearing completion and needed shows to justify its existence.

The Adelaide Festival Centre was the brainchild of Steele Hall, Liberal Premier of SA, who decided in 1968 that Adelaide should have a Festival Theatre. He was supported by Don Dunstan, then Leader of the Opposition, and by other distinguished persons. Lance Campbell, in *By Popular Demand, The Festival Centre Story*, recounts an excerpt from a 1967 conversation between Don Dunstan and Sir Robert Helpmann, Artistic Advisor to the Adelaide Festival of Arts in 1968 and Artistic Director in 1970:

> Now look here, Don, I'm running out of friends to invite to perform at the Festival because our venues are not adequate. I can't ask Benjamin Britten to perform *Les Illuminations* in Centennial Hall. We're scraping the bottom of the barrel here. You're going to have to plan for a proper centre for the Festival.

Don Dunstan succeeded Steele Hall in 1970 and made the Festival Theatre his top priority. The new edifice was not only to be the main venue for the biennial Festivals but also to house performances by local companies.

Australian Dance Theatre (ADT) (1965) and State Theatre Company (STC) (1975) were already established – an opera company would complete the performing arts trilogy.

The Festival complex design comprised a main multi-purpose theatre seating 1,983 and intended to accommodate symphony concerts, large plays and opera. The Playhouse, of 640 seats, was to be the mainstage for the STC and a smaller space, aptly known as the Space, could hold up to 500, depending on the way in which the flexible seating was arranged. The whole building reflected the government's intention to provide homes for large and small, home-grown and visiting, professional and amateur performances, and to provide an attractive and accessible centre that would appeal to the general public and encourage them to attend the venue for its own sake, as well as to see the shows.

There was more than a shade of rivalry with Sydney in the building of the AFC. The much-publicised Sydney Opera House was bedevilled with arguments ranging from petty squabbles to blazing rows, the most spectacular culminating in the dismissal of Jørn Utzon, the Danish architect who designed the complex. The Sydney Opera House took 18 years to build and cost $112 million.

The Adelaide project cost under $20 million and was completed in four years without major impediments, largely due to the Premier's close interest in the venture. Almost at the last minute before the opening Don Dunstan sat in the front row of the dress circle and found himself staring straight at the balcony rail – it was lowered pronto.

The wishes of the government and of the board and management of New Opera coincided perfectly in the matter of getting on with productions. In fact all involved with the establishment and the productions of New Opera look back on 1973 with amazement at both the ambitions and the achievements of that first year.

The company presented its first season of two one-act operas in May in the Union Hall at Adelaide University, followed by a single performance in the new Adelaide Festival Theatre as part of its acoustic tests in preparation for the grand opening on 23 June. In September two full-scale operas were seen in repertory and in October a single night of 'Opera-for-All' was mounted, both in the main theatre. In December two contemporary British music theatre works went on in the more intimate surroundings of Theatre 62. In all, a tally of three seasons, 16 performances, two major operas and six chamber ones. In addition, between March and July over 200 hundred performances were seen by 15,000 children in metropolitan and country schools.

Purcell's *Dido and Aeneas* and Ibert's *Angelique* were chosen for NOSA's first season, firstly for their popular appeal and secondly because they were regarded as being largely within the capabilities of local resources. The exceptions were Gaye MacFarlane, an appropriately buxom and sensual Angelique, and John Milson, director of the Ibert, both from Sydney. Both were conducted by Grahame Dudley. The double bill played first on 2–5 May in the Union Hall at the University of Adelaide to 'record attendances', according to New Opera's promotion brochure for the full season later in the year. On 8 May, the first performance of NOSA in the Festival Theatre contributed to the technical and acoustic testing process, playing to full (invited, of course) houses.

Opera critic Ralph Middenway reviewed *Dido* and *Angelique* in both theatres. From the Union Hall (*Advertiser*, 3 May) he developed a graceful conceit involving the 'larval' stage of IOG, and the 'chrysalis' of gradually growing professionalism in the 1972 seasons, leading into 'Now we have the butterfly'. He praised singers Patricia Price (Dido), Margaret McPherson (Belinda), John McKenzie (Boniface) and his 'noisy bitch of a wife' Gaye MacFarlane, directors Dean Patterson and John Milson, as well as designer Ian Brown. His final touch was 'And how nice to see Kathleen Steele Scott there, on stage, in such a lovely vignette part' namely, the gossip Madame Mathieu.

The same critic found that the move to the Festival Theatre brought 'new spaciousness' to Purcell's opera and opined that Ibert 'lost dramatically, gained musically'. He also referred to the 'most beautiful acoustics' and quoted seasoned Scottish baritone John McKenzie – 'This is the best opera house I have ever played in.' A tactful observation from a relative newcomer to Adelaide, but one not shared as the novelty of the theatre wore off.

The general euphoria over the new company and the new theatre carried the performances, and the fact that many of those on and off stage were way beyond their competencies was generally tolerated, if not ignored. This was the time to celebrate what had been achieved, not to complain about shortcomings. And after all, one of the ideals of the new company was to give the stage to local musicians, so they were at least entitled to have a go.

The theatre itself was not dealt with so charitably. There were naturally technical problems, but these could be sorted out by experience. More serious was the dull acoustics. Supposed to be able to accommodate both speech and music with equal clarity and resonance, the theatre proved unresponsive to the singers and players and gave the audience a pretty dull time, acoustically speaking. Admittedly, only a few of the singers in the May season possessed voices with enough power and projection to set the welkin ringing in a 1,983 seat theatre, but even those who did – Michael Lewis, Patricia Price, Gaye MacFarlane – felt and sounded as though they were singing into a fog.

To the time of writing, the Adelaide Festival Theatre's acoustic has been a continuing source of frustration for performers, audiences and critics who know that they are not getting the full natural beauty of the music played and sung there.

New Opera's stakes rose nationally with the release on 30 May of the EMI recording of *The Young Kabbarli*, funded with assistance from the Council for the Arts and from Commonwealth Assistance to Australian Composers. Patrick Thomas conducted the players and singers who had staged Margaret Sutherland's opera in the previous November, and the recording was made in the Matthew Flinders Theatre at Flinders University. The company proudly claimed a number of firsts – first Australian opera company to be commercially recorded, and Australia's first quadrophonic recording. Melbourne critic, Kenneth Hince, notoriously hard to please and on the whole not well disposed towards contemporary music, pointed out these achievements in his Classical Records column (*Australian*, 12 June) and praised the performers. 'The cast, and especially its three principal singers, Genty Stevens, John McKenzie and Dean Patterson, gives an honest and professional account of the music. The playing of the chamber orchestra under Patrick Thomas is admirable.' His summary of the work itself concludes that it is 'a stage essay in assimilation and race relations rather than an active and dramatic work.' He was highly critical of the libretto – 'it is flat and insipid. Instead of showing character in action, it preaches ... Nevertheless the opera is, from a musical point of view, a substantial achievement, and in Australia it is a rare pleasure to find it so handsomely recorded.'

In September, Rossini's *Count Ory* and Britten's *Albert Herring* went back-to-back in the Festival Theatre, three performances each.

The presence of fully professional conductors and directors brought about at least to some extent the transformation that had been hoped for. Richard Divall and Stefan Haag for Rossini, Georg Tintner and John Milson for Britten, were able to challenge and motivate the largely local casts, with results that moved several notches up from the *Dido* and *Angelique* season. Paul Ferris came from Sydney to sing the Count, being one of the few tenors in the country with the seven top Cs and two top Ds that the role demands on call. After the season had finished, he announced that next time he played the role he would charge 'by the top C' for his fee.

The decision to import artistic leaders and singers for the major roles drew some criticism. With a touch of scepticism, Ted Knez (*Advertiser*, 8 September) headed an article 'SA's budding opera has chosen to try to burst into bloom next week', reporting that Stefan Haag, director for *Count Ory*, claimed that 'New Opera lacked experience and knowledge' and should have employed a 'professional, experienced consultant – someone who has been through all levels of management, singing and production'. As the interview for this piece was obviously conducted during the period when Stefan Haag was rehearsing the Rossini, his comments might be taken as referring to his cast, only one of whom had previously played substantial roles as a professional in a theatre comparable in size to the Festival. The article suggests that NOSA's program was too ambitious, and that money spent on imports would be better used in training singers. Stefan Haag was probably right, but the excitement engendered in local singers and audiences by two full-scale operas could not have been equalled by lying low and running training programs.

Despite the director's complaints the rehearsal period and the performance season for *Count Ory* were among the happiest many seasoned participants can recall. The whole cast, chorus and principals alike, revelled in the eminently singable music and farcical plot. The public loved the humour of a pack of Adelaide's best known baritones and tenors kitted out as nuns – beards and boots and all – and the extremely attractive score.

Many in the audience who had seen SA's first *Herring* in 1968 were able to pride themselves and their state on having seen the Britten opera not only once but twice, well ahead of their cousins in Melbourne and Sydney.

Neither opera found full favour with the press. Ralph Middenway (*Advertiser*, 12 September) could not excuse the singers in *Count Ory* for remaining 'glued to the conductor all night' and found the characterisation uneven. 'Dean Patterson, Norma Hunter, Robert Dawe and Norma Knight and the chorus all had a good sing' was his luke-warm summary, but Margaret MacPherson 'tossed off her coloratura with nonchalance and facility'.

The critic was equally unimpressed with *Herring* (*Advertiser*, 13 September). His statement that 'a mismatch of characters with actions or words is pretty obvious' was substantiated with specific instances, but he conceded that David Brennan (Sid) and Judith Henley (Nancy) were 'just right'. Eric Maddison, although commended for his 'fine singing', was accused of failing to reveal that Albert is 'not an unconscious fool, but a painfully self-aware coward.' James Renfrey (*News*, 12 September) complained that 'the singing … did not reach a satisfactory standard often enough. If the voices had come anywhere near their possessors' acting abilities, we would have had something to crow about and to remember. Benjamin Britten's riotous opera calls for large delivery from all concerned and a small hall. Last night that was reversed.' With hindsight these comments can be taken as directed as much against the dull acoustics of the new theatre as against the efforts of the singers. It took some time for the truth to dawn. Our beautiful palace was not perfect after all.

These two operas were also ground breakers in that they were accompanied in the spacious, well designed pit – an undisputed source of local pride – by the SA Symphony Orchestra. At that time, the arrangement was specifically for that season, but in later years an agreement was reached that an allocation of the orchestra's time was to be set side for the opera company.

On 17 October, only one month after *Ory* and *Herring*, both major works requiring considerable resources of people and money, New Opera was back in the Festival Theatre. In the first half of 'Opera-for-All' the company's chorus and principals presented excerpts from operas. These were followed by a double bill exemplifying the company's artistic policy of presenting contemporary and Australian works. Hindemith's *There and Back* was directed by Justin Macdonnell with college lecturer Brian Chatterton conducting. Dean Patterson directed Australian James Pemberthy's *Ophelia of the Nine Mile Beach*, and, because the cast comprised members of the Adelaide Singers, Oliver O'Brien, their musical director at that time, was appointed to conduct. The engagement of this ensemble, several of whom had worked in *The Young Kabbarli* in October 1972, was designed to test the possibility that its members might become the permanent nucleus of the opera company, adding to their contractual agreements with the ABC to build up full-time jobs for them. The theory was promising, but as the prime talents of these people lay in their voices rather than in their acting ability the idea was not pursued any further.

In December of the same year came another contemporary double bill, this one even more experimental than Hindemith and Pemberthy. NOSA rounded off its first full year of operations with two pieces from the very forefront of innovative English music theatre.

Composer Melanie Daiken made her own selection of poems from Vladimir Mayakovsky, described in the program notes 'as the foremost poet of Russia's revolutionary era', for her frankly political *Mayakovsky and the Sun* (1971); Harrison Birtwhistle's *Down by the Greenwood Side* (1969), described as a Dramatic Pastoral, draws on the traditional Mummers' Play and other sources. Both were conducted by Peter Narroway, formerly of Adelaide and then working with Victoria State Opera, directed by visiting English mime artist Mark Furneaux and designed by Axel Bartz.

'New Opera scored a breakthrough . . . with the performance of two stimulating contemporary works from Europe' wrote Harold Tidemann (*Advertiser*, 12 December). As supportive as ever, he praised the 'presentation of these miniature operas which give an exciting glimpse of developments in music theatre on the other side of the world', singling out for special mention the 'droll and convincing' work of Genty Stevens and conductor Peter Narroway, 'who worked wonders with his orchestra of nine'. In her round-up of the year's activities Helen Covernton (*Sunday Mail*, 30 December) observed: 'New Opera came into being and gave this state its first taste of contemporary music theatre' – something of an overstatement for a company whose musical roots were almost exclusively in the twentieth century. Perhaps she meant at a professional level.

The program for this event began a practice that became customary. The names of the six members of the Board of Management (Chairman Richard Brown), the five of the Artistic Committee (Chairman Kathleen Steele Scott), New Opera staff, production staff, Theatre 62 staff and Mary Handley (Chairman) and her eight colleagues of the Subscribers Committee were published. Each group included at least one IOG stalwart, confirming the quality of their service in the old company and their right to a place in the new.

The schools team of four singers, pianist (Mary Handley) and stage manager (Laura Harrison) had full-time jobs through the middle half of the year playing specially written music dramas to children on their own turf. Peter Tahourdin's *Parrot Pie*, commissioned by New Opera, was directed by Alan Farwell, on secondment from the Education Department to complete an honours degree in music education, as part of his course requirements, and

Professor Kobalt and the Krimson Krumpet was the first of several of Jeff Carroll's pieces to entertain and enlighten large numbers of potential opera goers.

During the first two years of New Opera South Australia most of the major decisions concerning repertoire and artists were made by the Administrator, Justin Macdonnell. The Artistic Committee largely endorsed his proposals, though occasionally suggestions were initiated by the chairman, Kathleen Steele Scott.

One quite serious difference of opinion arose in mid 1973. Macdonnell proposed to the Artistic Committee that Stefan Haag be appointed to oversee all the artistic matters of the company, reasoning that he had very wide experience of all types of opera and music theatre and his versatility would be most appropriate for the company. The discussion became quite heated, as Macdonnell pressed his case with some passion. The Chairman called for a pause, during which several members went for a walk around the block. They returned with a polite but adamant refusal, feeling some anxiety lest they caused offence to the senior executive who had nurtured the company through its teething stages. Not at all. For the first of many times, they discovered that his resilience and adaptability matched his passion. By the next morning, he had a new plan ready to present, apparently feeling no animosity over his rejection.

But the experience imprinted on the Administrator and the administration the need for an artistic leader.

6

Off to the Moon and Back – 1974

☙

The idea of putting on *The Excursions of Mr Broucek* for the 1974 Festival was one thing – the reality was another. The first Janáček opera to be performed in Australia, rarely seen even in the composer's native Czechoslovakia, not published with an English translation, scores extremely difficult to obtain; but the story was so wonderfully fantastical – one act taking the hero to the moon, the other back to the Hussite wars in the fifteenth century.

Justin Macdonnell recorded the negotiations that led to this audacious decision (*Opera Australia*, March 1986). News that The Australian Opera would not be available for the 1974 Adelaide Festival of Arts brought a swift reaction in Adelaide.

> Much to the alarm of his colleagues and the Festival's Board of Governors, Artistic Director Anthony Steel turned to the infant state opera company – barely six months old – and proposed that they should fill the gap ... with Mozart's *Idomeneo*. With the brashness that only the newborn can muster the company replied that they would prefer to stage Janáček's *The Makropulos Case*. Steel immediately said that if it had to be Janáček then it had rather be *The Excursions*

Thomas Edmonds, Greg Dempsey and Marilyn Richardson,
The Excursions of Mr Broucek, 1974

of Mr Broucek. When the company replied that it was not exactly the opera on everybody's lips, Steel, with that combination of aplomb and tenacity which I trust will never desert him declared that 'that was exactly the point'.

The first task was to organise a small army of musically literate opera enthusiasts to write Norman Tucker's translation under the Czech text in a dismantled master score, which was then photocopied and re-assembled.

Stefan Haag was engaged to direct, partly on the strength of his happy association with the company for *Count Ory* in 1973, and the light touch he had shown in dealing with comedy. He decided to use a hippy setting for the moon act, and modified the text to allow for appropriate behaviour, such as was popular at the time among the flower people of the Haight Ashbury district in San Francisco. After considerable initial planning, but before rehearsals had begun, Haag became seriously ill and had to withdraw.

John Tasker took over, but felt uncomfortable with the hippy setting. Back to the drawing board went the text – the Haag bits were deleted and the original words restored.

Singers were brought from interstate – Marilyn Richardson, Paul Ferris, Lyndon Terracini – and also from overseas – Greg Dempsey and Thomas Edmonds both coming from London especially for the big tenor roles of Matej Broucek and Mazal – to complement locals Dean Patterson, Robert Dawe, Judith Henley and Noel Robbins. Australians, all of them.

Patrick Thomas conducted the SA Symphony Orchestra and the production was designed by Stan Ostoja-Kotkowski and Ross Anderson. The event, another milestone in New Opera's development, found favour with both the public and the press and attracted large and enthusiastic houses.

'One of the most delightful, funny, exciting, colourful and musical operas of the century' enthused Ralph Middenway (*Advertiser*, 12 March). The part of Broucek (Greg Dempsey) 'could have been written for him alone', Thomas Edmonds 'probably has never sung better' and Marilyn Richardson covered 'the whole spectrum from gossamer lyricism to anguished denunciation'. Described as 'unforgettable vignettes' were Robert Dawe's 'fancy critic and patron of the arts' and Dean Patterson's 'butterfly-catching Mandrake'. An unnamed but obviously well-informed writer (*Sunday Mail*, 17 March) hailed the 'small theatrical miracle taking place at the Festival Theatre', commending above all the 'stunning sets' of Stan Ostoja-Kotkowski, but expressing reservations about the 'sci fi lunar landscapes', where Broucek 'romps on silvery sunflowers and cavorts with moon nymphs and lads. These were ham and rather vulgar in their Everage chiffons with opening and shutting gladdies'. The writer may have found this scene 'jarring' – the audiences hooted with derision and delight. James Renfrey (*News*, 12 March) reported that 'The Festival Theatre was filled last night with people agog to follow *The Excursions of Mr Broucek*, a boozy nincompoop of Prague' and that the company's 'stakes had risen immeasurably because of it'.

The significance of this event was recognised by the attendance of critics from interstate and overseas. Their mainly favourable reviews brought the outstanding achievements of a very small, very new South Australian company to the attention of readers around Australia and in London. Katharine Brisbane

(*Australian*, 23 March), writing about the Festival generally, stated: 'The biggest local success has been New Opera's coup with *The Excursions of Mr Broucek*, which physically brought off a huge task of design and mounting at a level which has not been achieved before by a regional theatre company.' For Kenneth Hince (*Australian*, 21 March) *Broucek* 'came off on nearly all points, with great brilliance', and was ' the most substantial part' of the whole Festival program. He praised the 'unusually high calibre of singing across all the solo roles', comparing Greg Dempsey's 'rapscallion character' with Mozart's Masetto and Kodály's Háry János. Brian Hoad told his readers (*Bulletin*, 23 March) that New Opera 'leapt into the deep end' with *Broucek*, which 'whetted a thousand appetites with its blazing colours; it fired a thousand senses of adventure with its excitement'. According to Andrew Porter (*Financial Times*, London), 'Janáček's *Mr Broucek* was a performance that would be welcome in any part of the world'.

Co-incidentally, Myer Fredman, then first conductor and principal coach of Glyndebourne Festival Opera and musical director of its touring company, was in Sydney in January and February conducting *The Barber of Seville* for The Australian Opera. Through his connections with noted Australian tenor Ronald Dowd, Fredman's credentials had been circulated to the regional opera companies, so when NOSA's administrator received a phone call from the visitor from Glyndebourne expressing interest in 'talking to us' he was not totally unprepared. The two dined together after a performance in Sydney. 'I smelt a big chance, and invited him to stop over in Adelaide to see *Broucek* in the 1974 Adelaide Festival of Arts' is the way that Macdonnell remembers their first meeting.

Everything fell into place. Myer and Jeanne Fredman were introduced to Adelaide when the city was aglow with the success of New Opera's *Broucek* and graced by some very distinguished visiting artists – Paul Sacher with the Collegium Musicum of Zurich, Hans Hotter for masterclasses, the Jacques Loussier trio – and the Premier, Don Dunstan recited Ogden Nash's verses for *Carnival of the Animals* at the Adelaide Zoo. Peter Maxwell Davies was here with his Fires of London ensemble to perform the Festival commission *Miss Donithorne's Maggott*. By good fortune he and Myer Fredman attended *Broucek* on the same night and were among the backstage crowd that showered compliments on the cast and crew. Myer Fredman's interest increased from moderate to keen, but he was not immediately available, and in the meantime productions had to be nurtured.

Early in 1974, the position of Resident Conductor and Principal Coach (Chris Winzar promptly christened NOSA the Omnibus Company) was advertised nationally, and subsequently filled on a one year contract with option of renewal by Barry Golding, a Sydney musician with a good track record including working as repetiteur and conductor for The Australian Opera, Young Opera and Rockdale Opera.

Not surprisingly, after the extravagance of *Broucek*, NOSA's next production was modest. Donizetti's *Don Pasquale* played for seven nights in the Royalty Theatre, whose glories were distinctly faded. There was no pit, so the SA Symphony Orchestra, reduced to bare essentials, took up rows A and B as well as the small space in front of the stage. Dean Patterson played Pasquale, David Brennan was Malatesta and Judith Henley Norina. John Edmund directed and the designer was Ross Anderson. Barry Golding made his debut for NOSA as Resident Conductor and Principal Coach, the first person to take continuing charge of the company's musical affairs.

The company's first country tour for adult audiences, sponsored by the SA Arts Council, followed in June, with *Pasquale* playing in 16 different centres.

Although there must have been a formal constitution when NOSA was incorporated in January 1973, the earliest copy found to date is dated September 1974. Standard matters are covered, but an item of special interest is the requirement that a representative of the Company of Players be elected by their fellows to a position on the Board. Provision is made for a Program Planning Committee and an Advisory Committee for Development, which was to 'prepare recommendations for the development of the Association, with particular attention to the development of performance resources, and audience, and shall promote co-operation with other organisations for these purposes'. The term 'development' subsequently became common parlance for raising money from private sources, and it is useful to note that in 1974 the tacit assumption was that the company would be funded by government subsidies and box office returns.

New Opera took seriously its commitment to the education of both future and present patrons by running a workshop for 50 primary children to learn about opera production procedures through rehearsing and presenting a play based on Norman Lindsay's *The Magic Pudding* at Carclew arts centre, and by mounting a series of introductory public lectures on coming productions. Musicologist Elizabeth Wood spoke on '*Renard* and the Burlesque', Professor Andrew McCredie on 'The Opera and Monteverdi', composer Larry Sitsky on his opera *The Fall of the House of Usher* and Professor Wal Cherry on 'Brecht and Weill; A Study of Diverging Careers'. An innovation at the time, this practice eventually became common, if not general.

The final four months of New Opera's second full year of operation delivered an astonishing array of very new and very old music theatre pieces by major composers. It would appear that during this period the somewhat rigid and idealistic artistic policy laid down in January 1973 underwent a slight relaxation, as the program for the first season in May of that year records that the intention was to form 'a *Music Theatre Ensemble* presenting the best works of today with a sprinkling of the classics'. Pragmatism was beginning to leaven dogmatism.

Judging by the lack of enthusiasm in the reviews of Stravinsky's *Renard* and *The Fall of the House of Usher* by Australian composer Larry Sitsky, Stefan Haag's accusations that the company was being over-ambitious had some foundation. Ralph Middenway (*Advertiser*, 27 September) was prepared to allow that some of the problems lay in the theatre itself – the afore-mentioned distinctly unregal Royalty. Always worth reading for her feisty language, Helen Covernton reported (*Sunday Mail*, 29 September) that the Stravinsky was 'a multi-media eye-popper, combining colour film, rotisomatted chicken, provocative dance and evocative singing' and admired the 'gothic passion' in the 'chilling moments' of Sitsky's music.

Fortunately for New Opera the smaller performance areas of the Adelaide Festival Centre were nearing completion. In late October, the South Australian Theatre Company opened the 600-seat Playhouse with *The Three Cuckolds*, Commedia dell'Arte adapted into a play by Leon Katz. During the festivities the Amphitheatre was wall-to-wall with bands, jazz groups and popular performers, and in the flexible and readily adaptable Space the toddler opera company played *The Telephone* in four lunch-hours and by night Monteverdi's *Il Combattimento di Tancredi e Clorinda* (1642) and *The Seven Deadly Sins* by

Berthold Brecht and Kurt Weill. Barry Golding conducted all three, Dean Patterson directed the lunchtime entertainments, Justin Macdonnell directed and designed the Monteverdi and Wal Cherry directed its companion piece, which was designed by Silver Harris. Elder Professor David Galliver, Margaret MacPherson and Eric Maddison sang the baroque piece and the Weill cast was headed by Robyn Archer – the first time she had sung from a score, and her entry into a world in which she has become internationally respected. She still refers to *The Seven Deadly Sins* as a seminal step in the development of her stage career.

Noel Ancell (*News*, 29 October) described both the pieces as 'a morality play of a kind, and both were produced in an elegant, stylised manner that gave point both to the moral and the music, which was faultlessly played and sung . . . Stars of the evening were David Galliver, resplendent in ecclesiastical gear, and Robyn Archer, the power and cynicism of whose voice never failed to amaze.' He gave some of the credit to the venue. 'That the Space remained

Robin Archer (left), *The Seven Deadly Sins*, 1973

63

standing after the tumultuous applause from its first night audience says a lot for the architects too.'

`By October the news was out that Myer Fredman had accepted the position of Musical Director of the company, a decision that was met with some displeasure by Australian conductors offended at being overlooked in favour of a foreigner. Barry Golding was not able to accept an offer to stay on as Fredman's assistant and left the company to return to Sydney. Justin Macdonnell has commented that Golding 'did a good job', conducting his operas 'with flair and imagination. I would cheerfully have gone on working with him'.

NOSA turned again to Brecht and Weill in December for *The Little Mahagonny*, which was paired with *Novello*, a musical biography devised by Peggy O'Brien and Patrick Fraley. Lyndon Terracini and Gaye MacFarlane played alongside local singers Norma Knight, Daphne Harris and John Wood in both operas.

Brian Chatterton conducted, Chris Winzar directed *Mahagonny* and John Edmund *Novello*. The designer was Axel Bartz, and the elegant period costumes came from Laurence Blake, by courtesy of the South Australian Theatre Company.

The assessments of two local critics were in accord, both admiring the first half and unimpressed by the second. Helen Covernton (*Sunday Mail*, 8 December) praised 'the stunning production, beautifully sung, well acted and staged with ravishing cabaret flair' and found, although John Edmund directed the second half 'with authentic nostalgia', that 'the script was as dogged and earnest as Mr Novello himself'. Ralph Middenway (*Advertiser*, 4 December) confessed to being 'out of sympathy' with Novello's music, but admitted that 'it's a good line up of singers and probably very enjoyable if you like the idiom', and commended the Weill on both musical and dramatic grounds. Helen Covernton gave the company generally, though not 'its pompous and windy title', credit for its 'sense of style and a feeling for the times'.

The staff list for this program includes for the first time the name of Stuart Thompson, another Flinders University drama student who went on to carve out a significant career in opera and theatre management in Australia and the United States.

In addition to all of the above, NOSA managed to include in its second year a Northern Territory tour, presenting *The Telephone, Seven Deadly Sins* and *Professor Kobalt and the Krimson Krumpet.*

Plenty to crow about for New Opera in 1973–74, but the achievements were hard-won. Money flowed out faster than in; Secretary Kay Gallant had to go in person to the Department of Arts to collect salary cheques and they were cashed as late as possible on Friday afternoons, and at least once repetiteur Mary Handley and her team were stuck in a school waiting for their money while on tour. NOSA's office on Burbridge Road in the western suburb of Hilton was dreadfully scruffy – rats came to visit, the roof leaked, the only reliable toilet was across the road. But also across the road was a small church, converted to Theatre 62 by Chris Winzar and John Edmund. Just like New Opera, they were dependent on government grants and always short of money, always inventing ways to make the dollars go further, often calling on their mates in the better funded (though hardly affluent) State Theatre Company to help them out.

The theatre premises and persons were vital to both the practicalities and morale of the opera. The two companies shared (often over long lunches at the adjoining Red Garter restaurant) struggles, dilemmas, facilities and staff for both administration and production with an intimacy described by Macdonnell as being 'joined at the hip'. A quarter of a century on, he recorded that 'there was always a struggle and we relished it. It was what gave us energy. It was among the things that made us love the fight.'

7

Getting the Music Right – 1975

❦

Following his visit to Adelaide at the most auspicious, most welcoming time of the 1974 Adelaide Festival of Arts, when the city was in full artistic flight and New Opera was basking in the success of its fantastical *Broucek*, Myer Fredman's favourable first impressions crystallised into a decision to emigrate with his wife and two young sons.

Prior to taking up his appointment he was interviewed by Ted Knez (*News*, 9 December). 'Developing a distinct style personality for New Opera is the aim of Myer Fredman', the article began. (Actually NOSA already had a 'distinct style' – in fact, the most distinct style of any opera company in Australia.) Fredman elaborated. 'Style is like electricity. We know how it works, but we don't know what it is. And the only way to develop a style is to get under the skin of the company and bring it out. It means we will virtually have to eat, sleep and breathe as an entity. But I have not come here with the intention of injecting a style into the company. The ensemble feeling must evolve.' His aim included 'bringing about a balance between modern and more traditional works'.

In January 1975 he was appointed for three years to the position of Musical Director of New Opera, making his debut for the company in May with

Stravinsky's *The Soldier's Tale*, directed by Justin Macdonnell. It was paired for daytime (during the Youth Festival) with *The Little Mahagonny*, and in June for evening performances with *Dr Miracle* by Bizet, directed by Chris Winzar and conducted by Brian Chatterton, who by then had left his teaching position to become assistant to Fredman. The Bizet piece also saw the debut of Dennis O'Neill, who had been persuaded by Myer Fredman to follow him from England to Australia, where there was plenty of work for a capable and ambitious young tenor. James Renfrey (*News*, 26 June) thought the 'Great Musical Double' was a 'slice of great musical entertainment', wherein 'New Opera South Australia is disporting itself in the highest spirits ... Once again New Opera has shown us how it can encompass everything to do with operetta and music theatre. And the Space is admirable for the purpose'. Later in May Chester Schultz, a sterling repetiteur in *The Excursions of Mr Broucek*, conducted an ambitious program of Mozart, Beethoven, Stravinsky, Verdi, Wagner, Britten and Vaughan Williams by the New Opera Chorus in Way Hall.

The policy of performing operas outside the conventional repertoire continued in July in The Space with Janáček's *Diary of a Man Who Vanished*, sung by distinguished Australian tenor Ronald Dowd and accompanied by the young and gifted Stephen Walter, and *The Madrigal Show*, a baroque oddity by Banchieri. Helen Covernton (*Sunday Mail*, 6 July) admired the *Diary* but was 'stunned' by the Banchieri. 'It showed New Opera's burgeoning theatrical skills' as the cast became 'actors, tumblers, storytellers and dancers ... *The Madrigal Show* ... is a marvellous piece of inventive musical theatre – just the kind of thing that reinforces the importance of government subsidy'. She also commended Axel Bartz for his 'visually exciting set – a massive, multi-coloured clown mask, out of whose gaping orifices the performers belch in puffs of smoke'.

Just the kind of words that New Opera needed. Unfortunately the company was not attracting the audiences it needed to balance the books. The repertoire from the beginning of 1973 to July 1975 reflected exactly the policy laid down by the original artistic committee, but the blunt truth was that these intimate pieces had to be presented in appropriately intimate surroundings which could only accommodate small audiences. Chairman Hugh Cunningham and his board were forced to acknowledge that the gap between costs and income was widening. Larger audiences had to be attracted, and policy modified to take into account more popular taste.

The double bill of *The Turn of the Screw* by Benjamin Britten and Mozart's *Così Fan tutte* marked the point where idealism began to yield to pragmatism. In August, four performances of the former and six of the latter played in repertory in Her Majesty's Theatre. Prominent singers Ronald Dowd (Prologue and Peter Quint) and Ailene Fischer (Miss Jessel) came from Sydney for the Britten, and Dennis O'Neill (Ferrando), John Wood (Guglielmo), Marilyn Richardson (Fiordiligi), Norma White (Dorabella), Rae Cocking (Despina) and James Christiansen (Don Alfonso) were a strong Mozart cast. Myer Fredman conducted both, John Tasker directed and Peter Cooke (from the Queensland Theatre Company) designed *The Turn of the Screw*, and the production of Mozart's most entrancing opera was directed by Englishman Anthony Besch on exquisite sets with costumes by John Stoddart. The Britten orchestra, led by Robert Cooper, comprised a select group from the Adelaide Symphony Orchestra, and the University of Adelaide Chamber Orchestra, led by Wendy Thomson, played the Mozart. Apart from the 1974 Festival, not since the Flinders University season of *The Night Bell* and *Agrippina* in 1973 had such orchestral quality been assembled to accompany the opera.

The critics were pleased and the new Musical Director attracted considerable attention and not only for his conducting. Michael Harrison recalls an incident from *The Turn of the Screw* on 20 August 1975 in Her Majesty's Theatre.

A few minutes into the performance, the music stopped mid-bar. Daphne Harris (Governess) in her stride was left with mouth wide open.

Two seconds later: 'I will not conduct while you people bloody well talk and rustle your lolly papers.'

Stunned silence as conductor Myer Fredman leaves the pit.

The PA announcement: 'Ladies and gentlemen, tonight's performance will resume in a few minutes.'

To the relief of performers frozen onstage, the house lights come up and the stage darkens.

And true enough, ten minutes later the performance resumed without further incident. Maestro Fredman was warmly applauded on his return and at the end of the opera.

Norma Knight, Marilyn Richardson, *Così fan tutte*, 1975

Writing about the Britten, Dennis Atkins (*Sunday Mail*, 17 August) noted that 'Under the baton of Myer Fredman the orchestra, especially the pianist Stephen Walter, carried the show without missing a beat. They also blocked out some of the noise while Peter Cooke's superb sets were hurriedly being taken on and off'. The cast of *Così* attracted quite fulsome praise from several critics, the three women being particularly admired. James Renfrey called it (*News*, 22 August) 'an opera lover's dream'. These two productions were suffciently interesting to draw coverage from an interstate critic. Writing in the *Financial Review*, Nadine Amadio found the Britten 'an extremely moving production and the shape and sound of the music was stunning', and reported that 'This *Così* moved with wit and charm, was visually quite ravishing and was shaped with infinite musical elegance'. She added a most welcome general commendation and some advice. 'Nothing must be allowed to impede the progress of this company. Industry and business in South Australia could afford themselves a great deal of prestige by sponsoring and supporting a company which is bringing such recognition to the arts in their State.' Prophetic words, as it turned out. Non government sponsorship was virtually unknown in 1975, but within a few years raising money from private sources became a core activity of all Australian arts companies.

In September and October The Arts Council of South Australia ensured that the joys of this splendid production were not confined to the city but also made available to 18 different country centres. Brian Chatterton conducted from the piano and Dennis O'Neill repeated his success as Ferrando (good tenors are rare), Alan Horsfield (Guglielmo), David Brennan (Don Alfonso), Gwenyth Annear (Fiordiligi), Judith James (Dorabella) and Judith Henley (Despina) stepped into the other roles, most of them for the first time.

Further accolades were heaped on this *Così* in the following February when it received the National Critics Award for the best musical event in SA in 1975.

The witty and eye-catching printed program for *The Threepenny Opera* of Kurt Weill and Berthold Brecht, NOSA's final production in 1975, was proof of the company's rapidly growing sophistication. The front cover – signed 'By authority, B. Brecht Magistrate' – displays a mock-up of a WANTED notice for 'Burglar and Stick-up Man Captain Macheath, known as Mac the Knife', and on the back is a reproduction of an actual PROGRAM FOR THE ROYAL

CORONATION OF HIS MAJESTY KING GEORGE THE FIFTH, authorised by 'K. Weill, Organist'. All in black-and-white, this document was a striking advertisement for the event and demonstrates a leap forward in the company's appreciation of the power of print. (The program has become a collector's item.) Inside, the names of 41 people involved in the company's administrative and artistic operations were listed. Hugh Cunningham was Chairman of the seven-member board, Mr Justice Charles Bright headed the newly-founded New Opera Foundation, and Mary Handley led the Subscribers' Committee. Justin Macdonnell's administrative staff of six included Russell Mitchell, Stuart Thompson and Lorna Matthews, Musical Director Myer Fredman was supported by repetiteur David King and chorus master Chester Schultz, and Stage Manager Frank McNamara had three assistants. The sets, costumes and properties were executed in the New Opera Workshop, presided over by Jim Coogan and his seven-strong team. In only three years the family-and-friends IOG, where everybody did everything, had burst open to embrace specialists in every aspect of opera production. Continuity with NOSA's roots was preserved by IOG's Kathleen Steele Scott, Mary Handley, Laura Harrison and Meredith Patterson.

Wal Cherry, Professor of Drama at Flinders University, directed the production, and John Willett, an English authority on Brecht, colla-borated on the 'production

Threepenny Opera program, 1975

conception'. Myer Fredman conducted, Silver Harris Ewell was the designer and Tessa Bremner arranged the dances. The strong cast included David Brennan (Macheath), John Wood and Gwenyth Annear (Mr and Mrs Peachum), Patsy Hemingway (Polly), Robyn Archer (Jenny) and Dennis O'Neill (Sergeant Major). Ralph Middenway (*Advertiser*, 2 December) praised the concept, the 'marvellous warehouse cum Wingfield dump set and some nicely understated dances'. Both he and another critic (*Sunday Mail*, 7 December) were impressed by the overall ensemble strength, the latter singling out 'the Myer Fredman/ Wal Cherry combination, who between them produce a piece of entertainment which is pleasing both to the ear and to the eye'. Ian McIntosh (*News*, 2 December) found it 'visually rather magnificent' but

> too often rather a bore … In its battle to convince people that opera is a delightful experience for all segments of the community, it would seem to me that New Opera has gone a little too far this time – with unfortunate results … The reasons why it offers patrons only a pennyworth of entertainment are, firstly, the decision to produce it, secondly its length and lack of credibility and thirdly it just is not suited to the talents available.

New Opera's promise to support Australian composers with commissions and performances was honoured with a double bill in the 1976 Adelaide Festival. Larry Sitsky and George Dreyfus – neither of them known for his reticence in dealing with matters political and scatological – chose subjects designed to shock and mock. *Fiery Tales* combined Chaucer's *The Miller's Tale* with an equally lustful story from Boccaccio's *Decameron*; for *The Lamentable Reign of King Charles the Last* librettist Tim Robertson concocted what director Chris Winzar described as something between a law students' revue and Monty Python. The casts for both included NOSA regulars as well as Sydney baritone Howard Spicer.

Audiences in the Scott Theatre were somewhat bamboozled by the vulgarity, and many were offended at seeing and hearing their sacred cows treated with such blatant disrespect. 'DW' (*Sunday Mail*, 28 March) was totally dismissive of both pieces, referring to 'New Opera's ill-chosen offering for the Festival', and summing up *Lamentable Reign* thus; 'As an end of term school romp it was excellent; as a piece of opera, a major offering for the festival, it was pathetic.'

And: '*Fiery Tales* ... left me cold. The sight and sound of copulation and urination to atonal music left a lot to be desired.' James Renfrey fumed (*News*, 24 March) about the Dreyfus piece 'For crass bad taste, bad humour and an overall adolescence [it was] unmatched in my experience' and berated librettist Gwen Harwood who had 'brewed' a 'series of bare bottoms, visits to the lav, and lewd jokes'.

Sydney critic Maria Prerauer (*Australian*, 25 March) was vastly entertained, finding both pieces

> genuinely funny, high-spirited and bursting with vitality ... Chris Winzar's Monty Pythonesque direction, Axel Bartz's colourful designs and Myer Fredman's racy conducting of the chamber orchestras all worked together to provide both operas with pace and gusto. And there is not a weak link in the cast of top professional actor-singers.

She concluded with a barb: 'The sort of thing The Australian Opera for all its expensively mounted productions has been missing out on too often of late.' John Cargher (*Bulletin*, 10 April) found it all 'delightfully daffy' and noted 'there is a degree of undergraduate chaos which needs pruning, but there is such a wealth of comic invention and gloriously bad puns that criticism is muted'. Cargher took pains to ensure that his readers knew these booked-out pieces were by Australian composers. Distinguished visiting critic Andrew Porter reported (*Advertiser*, 27 March) that Reg Livermore's work in *Betty Blokkbuster Follies* 'points down one of the paths ... which modern opera is travelling. The two one-act operas premiered by New Opera SA took some clumsy, not especially talented, steps in the same direction.'

During the same Festival, The Australian Opera played its Australian première of Alban Berg's *Wozzeck*, which attracted a substantial number of patrons from interstate. They and local opera supporters had plenty to argue over with two highly controversial shows on offer – but also something to boast about. Perhaps they did not make great dinner table capital from Sitsky and Dreyfus, but the sets and costumes of the TAO *Wozzeck* were destroyed in a warehouse fire soon after the Adelaide season, and not until 1999 did the rest of the country see this twentieth-century classic.

NOSA broke with tradition in May by taking a production of *La Bohème* on a tour of high schools and colleges in outer suburban centres – Oakbank, Salisbury, Christie's Beach – before showing the opera in the city. The accompanist was David King, a highly gifted musician at the beginning of an outstanding career in theatre music, and costume designer Laurence Blake made a cameo appearance as a waiter. Cigarettes were supplied by Rothman's Australia.

In the wind were three matters that would give NOSA its first major shake-up. After three years as the company's official, and almost one more as unofficial, chief executive, Justin Macdonnell was ready for a change. He had summarised his decision to move on thus. 'I had been in Adelaide for eight years. The Whitlam era had just ended. I had a gut feeling that the Dunstan era was soon to follow.' (Fortunately his pessimism was unwarranted.) 'I knew (suspected) that the days of what I most wanted to do were numbered – i.e. contemporary theatre.' In December he accepted a job offer in Sydney. Twenty-five years later, he recorded his 'proudest achievements' with New Opera as follows:

1 Creating for just two brief years an ensemble that could do music theatre at such a level (doing weekly movement classes as well as music preparation), that would try anything without complaint, that led one actor seeing them in rehearsal to ask: 'Are they actors or dancers?' and I could say: 'No, opera singers'.

2 Casting Robyn Archer in *The Seven Deadly Sins* and thereby launching a career and a friendship that remains to this day.

3 Presenting so much Australian work and contemporary work.

4 Leaving when I did.

He could and should have added that his efforts to secure the future of the company came to fruition in July, after his departure, when the SA government agreed to confer the status of a statutory authority on what then was re-named The State Opera of South Australia.

Coincidental with Macdonnell's urge to move on was a similar need felt by Ian D. Campbell, at that time working for the Music Board of the Australia Council as Senior Music Officer. His wide and varied background included comprimario roles with The Elizabethan Trust Opera (later The Australian Opera) and a degree majoring in history, and his work with the Council entailed visiting the regional opera companies and familiarising himself with their artistic and financial dealings.

His appointment at NOSA – on the recommendation of Macdonnell – was as General Manager, a significant change from his predecessor's title of Administrator. The difference between the personalities of the two men is reflected in how they chose to name their positions.

Campbell was appointed on 12 May 1976. On 21 May he wrote a foreword to the brochure announcing the subscription program for that year. (Justin Macdonnell gives Chris Winzar the credit for 'shaping the shows that made that [transition] time so exciting and, at its best, so anarchic'.) In his foreword, Campbell was also able to announce the arrival of Adrian Slack (invited to Australia through his Glyndebourne connections with his compatriot Myer Fredman) as Director of Productions, and to acknowledge the assistance of the Subscribers' Committee with the costs of his travel.

The new GM had some breathing space in his first two months while the company dealt with school holiday workshops of *The Moonrakers* and *Mr Punch*, city and country tours of *Professor Kobalt's Kinetic Contraption* and a concert by company members in the Art Gallery based on the letters and music of Mozart.

In July NOSA was back on the stage with a bold – anarchic? – season running three frankly experimental pieces in repertory. *Never the Twain*, a modern show devised from the writings of Rudyard Kipling and Bertholt Brecht with music from Weill, Eisler, Dessau and other suitable sources, alternated with Chabrier's barely known, archetypically nineteenth-century *Ignorance is Bliss?* and *Festino*, a baroque madrigal opera by Banchieri, probably intended for concert per-formance but moulded for this occasion into music drama. These events not only opened the eyes and ears of NOSA's audiences but also gave local direc-tors, designers and musicians opportunities to create their own shows.

For *Never the Twain*, John Willett compiled the material, David King organ-ised the music and Wal Cherry directed. The large cast included Robyn Archer and the Sydney actor John Gaden.

Meanwhile, the case for Her Majesty's Theatre becoming a permanent home for State Opera was simmering. An Editorial (*News*, 20 August) brought to public attention the fact that the present owner had decided to sell its

Australian chain, and promoted the claim of the company 'which has emerged as a major force on the cultural scene'.

When Campbell took NOSA on, he knew it was in a parlous state financially, with a deficit of $80,000 on a turnover of $300,000. Things were really grim. As he described the situation in later years: 'In the first two weeks I was here there was no money for salaries. The grant was used up, salaries (for singers) were paid by staff. I put in $50 of my own money.' (As had done Justin Macdonnell and Kathleen Steele Scott before him.) 'We had overdrafts at the bank.' He blamed the situation on poor book-keeping, and claimed that the Board was aware of some – though not all – of the problems.

Prior to the opening of the July season (a curate's egg if there ever was one), he had gone public about the company's support base. John Kirby reported him (*Sunday Mail*, 20 June) as saying that subscriptions were down a third on the same period last year. The new GM was well aware that the fall-off in subscribers contributed to a level of debt that was insupportable and could lead to the demise of the company.

On 8 August his immediate fears, at least, were allayed. The Premier, Don Dunstan, announced that the company was to be known henceforth as the State Opera of South Australia, and to become a statutory authority established by act of parliament.

The program for the August season of *La Bohème*, the first production of State Opera, carried a glowing – perhaps slightly overdone – endorsement by Don Dunstan. He was right that New Opera had made a significant mark on music theatre in SA, but the claim that 'Its standards and achievements are admired throughout the world' was something of an overstatement. However the Premier's reference to the 'professionalism, vigour and imagination' of NOSA and his certainty that under SOSA 'its reputation will be further enhanced' was not misplaced.

A week before the opening of *La Bohème* a substantial article appeared in the press (*Advertiser*, 7 August). Arts Editor Shirley Despoja described the ramshackle state – two converted churches and a condemned building – of State Opera's rehearsal, wardrobe and administration premises, and (tactfully prompted by the new GM) flagged the prospect of Her Majesty's Theatre, the venue for the imminent season, becoming the company's home. 'Anyone got a million to help out?', she queried. Her article was the first public move in a campaign that three years later resulted in Her Majesty's being re-furbished and re-opened as The Opera Theatre.

La Bohème saw the return to Adelaide of Gwenyth Annear (Mimi) and Thomas Edmonds (Rodolfo), both of whom had built successful careers in England and Europe. Both had strong family ties in Adelaide, but there is no doubt that the existence of a fully professional opera company in their home town was a strong incentive for them to resume residence here. Their companions as the opera's lovers were James Christiansen (Marcello) and Patsy Hemingway (Musetta); Keith Hempton (Colline), John Wood (Schaunard), David Brennan (Benoit and Alcindoro) and Robert Angove (Parpignol) completed the strong and entirely local cast. Myer Fredman conducted and also wrote a new English translation, Chris Winzar directed, Silver Harris-Ewell designed the sets and Laurence Blake the costumes. The Adelaide Symphony Orchestra appeared by courtesy of the Australian Broadcasting Commission. Warren Bourne (*Advertiser*, 19 August) praised all aspects of the production and the music, as well as the singers' articulation. 'All members of the cast made it their business to be not just audible but also intelligible. Consequently the humanity and immense variety was astonishing.' He concluded his comments on the core quartet with: 'Their technical assurance and emotional conviction needs only a more uninhibited lyrical expansion to be exhilarating.' John Kirby (*Sunday Mail*, 22 August) praised the principal quartet and the orchestra, but found that 'Chris Winzar's direction . . . is quite unremarkable, the chorus sloppy and Silver Harris-Ewell's set reminiscent of a napalm-devastated village'. Ralph Middenway (*Australian*, 20 August) was clearly unimpressed by the work itself, but had a word of praise for Gwenyth Annear for 'dying musically, quietly and simply'.

Campbell missed no opportunity to bring his company to public notice. His letter to the editor entitled 'Orchestral hurdle for Opera' (*Advertiser*, 15 August) took local music writer Dr Enid Robertson to task over her misinterpretation of his comments on the Delibes opera *Lakmé* and extended his case to argue for better provision of orchestral services for SOSA. 'Unless a second orchestra is established in this state or current resources are rationalised to a point where they are made more readily available to bodies such as ours, the growth of operatic and choral activities will be greatly restricted.' Meanwhile, his persuasive powers had worked on another front. In early September the state government bought Her Majesty's Theatre for a reported $440,000 with the intention that it become SOSA's permanent home for both performance and administration.

Press coverage for the company's final production for 1976 began with an unprecedentedly extensive full page feature in the *Advertiser*'s Saturday Review. Shirley Despoja wrote a teasing story (*Advertiser*, 20 November) about a rehearsal of the forthcoming production, Cimarosa's *The Secret Marriage*, managing to cover not only the essentials of the plot and the deviousness of its characters but also sketch in the person and philosophy of the director, Adrian Slack, and slip in a plug for the decision to give the company a new home. Despoja's enthusiasm for NOSA at this time was typified by her willingness to attend a rehearsal rather than merely conduct an interview.

The Secret Marriage played in the Scott Theatre, not an ideal venue for a classical opera, but apparently none of the critics was offended. Myer Fredman conducted the University of Adelaide Chamber Orchestra, Axel Bartz designed, and the cast comprised John Wood, Patsy Hemingway, Dennis O'Neill, David Brennan, Norma Knight and Gwenyth Annear. Liz Wood (*Advertiser*, 24 November) praised them all, and added that wardrobe supervisor 'Laurence Blake's footman deserves his applause for the most elegant scene changes and footwork seen below stairs for many a year.' Ralph Middenway's review (*Australian*, 1 December) was coloured by resignation: 'Maybe it's inevitable that the SA company will have to shelter a bit more behind the popular reper- toire ... But with luck ... the State Opera won't completely lose its spirit of adventurousness and will maintain its resourceful approach to low budget limitations.'

In another sign that Campbell's sights were set wide, he secured an engage- ment for *The Secret Marriage* to be played at the Perth Festival in February 1977, causing, according to the gossip, some chagrin to the local West Australian Opera Company. Shirley Despoja went too, and reported (*Advertiser*, 14 February) that the production had been further refined since its debut at the Scott Theatre, that the cast excelled themselves, that Myer Fredman's adap- tation of the score for four violins, two cellos, a clarinet and a harpsichord was well suited to the tiny pit and that 'Axel Bartz's simply clever, revolving doll's house set got applause twice from the audience'.

With an interstate visit – claimed to be the first by an Australian regional opera company – stage one of the professional company's existence ended. Through President Kathleen Steele Scott, Board chairman Hugh Cunningham and members Richard Brown and Brian Hunter, and Subscribers' Committee members Mary Handley, Kay Gallant and Laura Harrison connections to State Opera's predecessors were maintained, ensuring that any future changes would be made in the light of past experience.

8

New Brooms Sweep Clean as Long as They Are New – 1977–80

aving worked through the plans laid by their predecessors, by 1977 Musical
Director Myer Fredman and General Manager Ian D. Campbell were free to
put their own stamp on repertoire as well as on standards and style, both of
which had changed radically since their appointments in January 1975 and
April 1976 respectively.

Mixed with regret that the original policy of New Opera SA had proved
unrealistic was justifiable pride – the annals show that of the 35 operas
(including schools' programs) staged during 1973–6, 25 were from the twentieth century, a remarkable record, and one which gives South Australia the
right to claim greater acquaintance with contemporary opera than any other
state in the country.

The Fredman-Campbell alliance showed admirable balance in its repertoire
selection for 1977, and with two of the three choices retained previous principles. The Savoy operas of Gilbert and Sullivan – not even the blatantly anti-
establishment *HMS Pinafore* – would never have reached the stage during the
Macdonnell era, but they were likely to attract full houses, especially with the
added lure of a relatively famous television star. Mozart, on the other hand, was

certainly on the previous list of approved composers, and *Don Giovanni* was a popular choice for its wonderful music and the sexual and political relevance of its plot. Monteverdi's study of sex and politics, *The Coronation of Poppea*, was the only risk, both the composer and the work being virtually unknown to most opera patrons, but it would not have been out of place in New Opera's philosophy.

In the event, these three operas were well received by both audiences and critics, and set the company well on the way to building a solid base of loyal supporters who were persuaded that their interests were of paramount importance. This new approach replaced the earlier policies, which had been more concerned with shaping than with satisfying public taste.

One of Campbell's stated aims on assuming office was to engage professional directors and designers in place of the locals who had fulfilled these functions in about three-quarters of the repertoire of the previous three years. He was also determined to debunk the conviction that operas needing orchestras and choruses were beyond the company's means, and set about proving that the Adelaide public would support local singers as well as imported ones, as long as they were good enough.

For the 1977 program, Myer Fredman conducted and Adrian Slack directed all three operas, and the designers were John Cervenka (already known for his work with the State Theatre Company) for *Poppea*, Jim Coogan for *Pinafore* and Axel Bartz, who had been frequently engaged under the previous regime, for *Don Giovanni*.

The casts were all Australian, most of them regulars on Adelaide's stages. Exceptions were Greg Dempsey, making a second return home from working in Europe to sing Nero – his first had been for *Broucek* in 1974, and his next engagement following *Poppea* was for the British première of the same piece at Covent Garden – and Eileen Hannan, fitting her Poppea in between roles in Glyndebourne and Wexford.

Advertiser Arts Editor Shirley Despoja excelled herself with preliminary teasers about each opera, homing in on aspects of the works and the productions that were likely to appeal not only to opera buffs but also to the uninitiated who might be encouraged to dip their toes in the water. About *Poppea* (*Advertiser*, 27 April) she gave a layman's account of how the bare bones of

Monteverdi's score are fleshed out by the musicians, and nearer the opening (1 July) produced a piece about Nero and Poppea tap dancing, complete with action photograph, and quoting them as 'looking forward to playing their "naughty" roles'. For *Pinafore* she gate-crashed a dress rehearsal where Sir Joseph Porter, played by Edward Woodward (then famous as the TV character Callan), was tackling the perilous business of climbing the rigging in monocle, cocked hat and sword. Her story ('One Flew over the Poop Deck', *Advertiser*, 10 September) is still an hilarious read, and probably helped to attract the record audience of 22,000 to this joint production of SOSA and the Adelaide Festival Centre. But it also had a serious vein, revealing that behind the polished product seen by the public is a huge amount of practice, often involving considerable physical risk. Most critics were well entertained by *Pinafore*, but John Kirby (*Sunday Mail*, 18 September) found the production 'depressingly effete – it lacks guts'. His most generous praise was for 'that splendid comedian, John Wood (Captain Corcoran)' whose song 'Never Mind the Why and Wherefore' was 'the highspot of the production'. Of the star, Kirby wrote that he 'handles himself well as befits an actor of this stature, but apart from the big name gimmick, it was a long way to come for such a small slice of the action'.

Behind Woodward's engagement there was another story that does not seem to have made the press at the time but was freely bruited around. On a previous visit to Adelaide, the possibility of him appearing in a Shakespearean tragedy with the State Theatre Company was discussed. When he was offered a contract, he asked his agent for a copy of the script, expecting *King Lear*. Instead, *HMS Pinafore* landed in his lap. Unfortunately Ian Campbell was unable to confirm the story. While agreeing that it is amusing, he replied to a question on the matter that 'Woodward never mentioned any such thing to me ... The deal ... was that he was to sing Sir Joseph Porter for a set fee, plus a share of the profits once we reached a certain figure. In return ... he would co-operate on advertising, interviews, and would do a TV commercial promoting the show, all of which he did splendidly. He was a lot of fun to have around.'

As a preliminary to the November season of *Don Giovanni*, the Friends of the State Opera arranged a public lecture in Edmund Wright House. The occasion was booked out well in advance, and began a practice that has been maintained ever since and has been a major factor in the promotion of public acceptance and increasing familiarity with opera. Shirley Despoja also helped the promotion with 'Search for the Lost Chord' (*Advertiser*, 3 November), showing Myer Fredman testing out the suitability of various planks, poles and beams to represent the 'stomp, thump or bump (with resonance, please)' for the Commendatore's statue making his ghostly entry.

Ralph Middenway (*Australian* 15 November) took issue with the production, especially the lighting, and pointed to the lack of authority as the main flaw in the production. John Kirby (*Sunday Mail*, 13 November) agreed about the production, finding it 'dull. As a piece of theatre it just does not make it' and blaming both Axel Bartz's set and Adrian Slack's direction for the fact that 'The cast performs woodenly and this lack of animation makes a long opera seem too long.'

In addition to these three major seasons, in its first year the Fredman-Campbell alliance ran a concert entitled 'Opera – an Irrational Entertainment' in Edmund Wright House in conjunction with Musica Viva in July. In place of school tours, in May SOSA's Education Officer Victoria Owens managed a song quest, inviting young people to sing for a group of professional judges, and in October organised the Sing-Your-Head-Off festival which attracted 1500 primary school children. In the city, the year was rounded off with *Gilbert Versus Sullivan: The Fight of the Century*, a 'sparkling presentation ... which gathered momentum after a dull beginning' according to Harold Tidemann (*Advertiser*, 12 December). In conjunction with the Arts Council of SA the show toured to the outback, and Shirley Despoja, who was clearly enjoying her association with opera and opera people went along. 'Opera on the Boil' (*Advertiser*, 10 December) introduced her readers to a new version of the form way out west of Port Augusta in 40 degree heat. 'Punka opera is when there's nothing between sanity and blood boiling but six punka fans stirring the thick hot air like a pudding.' As with many of this perceptive writer's articles, she wove into her piece the trials and tribulations of the performers – pianist David McSkimming had a chair with 'at least two good legs', the singers 'were dressed to kill in Victorian gear' – as well as facts and figures about the 'sad, stunted cereal crops on the way into Wudinna', and the singers' sympathy with the farmers – 'David Brennan had said suddenly "It seems like cheek for us to come to a place like this and expect people to pay money to see a show"'.

Performing was over for 1977, but SOSA was still being mentioned in despatches. In his book *Opera and Ballet in Australia* John Cargher praised New Opera for its lack of pretension. Reviewing the volume, William Reschke (*Sunday Mail*, 27 November) failed to disentangle Cargher's elaborate metaphors of sacred cows and dinosaurs but his intention was favourable. (Incidentally, Cargher's account of the origins of Intimate Opera was larded with inaccuracies, as were most early attempts to tell the story.) SOSA also made the paper (*Advertiser*, 17 December) with a report that Ian Campbell had auditioned singers in London for roles with SOSA. The Actors and Announcers Equity Association complained that Australian singers were being overlooked, and threatened to refuse to allow union tickets to overseas singers. Myer Fredman and others were quoted explaining that particular voice and person-ality types were being sought to match specific roles, that the practice was normal worldwide, and that the presence in London of the General Manager was a logical opportunity for him to hear and see singers outside Australia.

But before the year was really over came a significant announcement. Historically, opera in South Australia had depended largely on touring companies, starting with Mr Coppin's English Opera Company in 1856 and continuing with the likes of Signor and Signora Bianchi's Grand Italian Opera Company in 1861. J.C. Williamson's English Opera Company made its first foray into SA in 1881 and the same entrepreneur showed his wares nearly 60 times between then and 1969. From 1962 the Elizabethan Trust Opera Company shared credits with him, and by 1970 the national company had settled its title as The Australian Opera (TAO) and came to Adelaide almost every year thereafter. Naturally there was some rivalry between the local and national companies, as well as concern about the escalating costs of both, so the announcement by Peter Hemmings and Ian D. Campbell, General Managers of The Australian Opera and State Opera of South Australia respectively, that in 1978 the two companies would present a joint season of five operas was generally approved. Subscribers were wooed with promises of five operas for the price of four, guaranteed seats not only for 1978 but also for subsequent years and a line-up of singers, directors and designers that put SOSA regulars alongside, in democratic alphabetical order, many of the best in the land. Conductors were listed as Myer Fredman for all the SOSA productions and for TAO its Musical Director Richard Bonynge, making his first appearance in Adelaide since the Sutherland-Williamson season in 1965 which had helped to persuade him and his illustrious wife Joan Sutherland that Australia could match the standards of production that they had become accustomed to in their joint international careers.

The deal offered decent nourishment, spread out over the year. From SOSA *The Marriage of Figaro* in May, *La traviata* in June and a lesser known Puccini, *La Rondine* in August, all in the Opera Theatre. TAO would mount *Nabucco* and *The Mikado*–later changed to *The Yeomen of the Guard*, with William Reid conducting–in the Adelaide Festival Theatre in October. In addition, each company would have a presence in the Adelaide Festival of Arts–Tippett's *Midsummer Marriage* from the home team and Scarlatti's *The Triumph of Honour* from the visitor's Opera Studio. The announcement predicted a further, expanded season (including *Aida*) for 1978, and considered the possibility of State Opera visits to Sydney, joint productions and an increasing exchange of artists.

For the 1978 Festival State Opera maintained its tradition of producing Australian premières of major twentieth-century operas, this time at a cost of $100,000. *Midsummer Marriage*, with words and music by Michael Tippett, was first performed in 1955. The Grove Concise Dictionary of Music describes it as 'a pastoral, a modern morality and a mystery play of psychic growth', and its similarities to *The Magic Flute* are noted. The composer made a special visit to Adelaide for this Festival to see his opera and also to attend concerts of his orchestral works.

Tippett's highly idiosyncratic, often convoluted text provided much fodder for serious discussion amongst those who attended the performances, and ulti-mately the only conclusion reached was that there were many possible inter-pretations of what it actually meant. For David Gyger (*Theatre Australia*, May 1978) it was 'a highly intellectualised parable involving surreal shifts of time and place from the here and now to some vaguely located time and place', for Neil Jillett (*Age*, 27 February), the libretto was a 'mixture of Tolkien's *Hobbit* stories, Mozart's *The Magic Flute* and *The Teddy Bears' Picnic*'.

Judgments flew freely on whether Tippett had succeeded in his stated aim 'to try to transfigure the everyday with a touch of the everlasting', but the singers and the dancers, choreographed by Jonathon Taylor from the Australian Dance Theatre, were generally admired, and Alan Brissenden (*Advertiser*, 27 February) devoted a whole review to them. Kenneth Hince, not given to enthusing over contemporary music, was mainly complimentary, finding the event 'another major and considerable achievement for the company and one in which it should take considerable pride'. Maria Prerauer (*Australian*, 27 February) was clearly sceptical about the work, describing it as 'a cross between Mozart's *Magic Flute* and Shakespeare's *Midsummer Night's Dream*' but praised the performers without exception.

Among the adverse criticisms were complaints that the design did not follow the composer/librettist's strict instructions, ignoring the sense of ritual that pervades the piece and failing to match the physical vision to the musical one. In an interview after the opera's opening, Tippett declared himself well pleased with the production, describing it as the best he had seen. Later, when questioned on the fact that his own wishes had not been followed, he confessed that he was nearly blind, and that although he had been given very good seats he could hardly see the stage. And that he never reads the critics.

In April, Campbell continued to extend his managerial influence outside South Australia. Singers Patsy Hemingway, Angela Denning, Roger Howell and Mario Alafaci, all SOSA regulars, and pianist Bronwyn Elsegood took 'Opera – an Irrational Entertainment' and 'Gilbert versus Sullivan', both well received in Adelaide, to Tasmania, including King Island and Flinders Island, two places with very small populations, for twelve performances. A Taswegian thought it likely that there would have been more cows and mutton birds than people in the audience.

Also in April the company announced that it would form its own orchestra in order to avoid the problems caused by having to juggle opera seasons around orchestral concerts calling on the same players. For some years various proposals had been emerging for a second orchestra, at least one dating back to 1975, but none had been of sufficient substance to attract a definite commitment of government subsidy. Among the unsuccessful bids was State Opera's original plan, designed to operate from August 1977, for a separate orchestra which would be available mainly for opera and dance. Meanwhile, Adelaide musician John Russell was on the threshold of a career as entrepreneur. In 1976 Russell had formed the Adelaide Chamber Soloists (later Orchestra) with basic government support. Abandoning the idea of forming a permanent chamber orchestra for concerts and pit work, and with Russell's assistance, State Opera followed his model of hiring the best players available for specific engagements. By April 1978 the company had formed a band of 36 players out of its own resources, and announced that its debut would be for *The Marriage of Figaro* in May. When the news was made public, Ian Campbell predicted that SOSA's initiative would lead, within a few years, to a second orchestra. His crystal ball was telling him what he wanted to hear. There is no second orchestra today, but the Adelaide Symphony Orchestra has a permanent commitment to servicing the company's orchestral needs. The background to this current policy can be traced to SOSA's manoeuvres as early as 1977, and Russell still likes, quite rightly, to claim some of the credit.

Advance bookings for *Figaro* set a new box office record for SOSA, no doubt assisted yet again by Despoja's perky promotion piece (*Advertiser*, 1 April): 'The last time Tom McDonnell saw Eileen Hannan he died in her arms'. It was an irresistible introduction to the virginal but wordly-wise Susannah and the lascivious Count determined to exercise his *droit de seigneur* in the upcoming opera. Also included was a valuable tip for young artists – Hannan revealed that the most important service any singer can perform for a dying colleague is to 'hold his head up so he can see the conductor'.

The critics were reasonably happy, giving special notice to Roger Howell's debut Figaro and to Eileen Hannan's Susannah. James Renfrey (*News*, 5 May) was blunt about the State Opera Orchestra, whose 36 players, led by veteran Mary Pascoe and including John Russell in the violins, were listed in the program. 'Myer Fredman made the best of his resources. and it was not his fault if occasionally the tone was pinched and the intonation down at heel. But he should have ensured that sound between stage and pit synchronised.' A new name appeared as Chorus Master – Jon Draper, an Englishman who had come to Adelaide as director of the newly formed Woodville Special Interest Music School but had moved quickly from classroom to conducting when he spotted an opening.

The program for *La traviata* lists a small army of staff and elected officers. Topped by what was being referred to as 'the triumvirate' of Fredman, Campbell and Slack – though there was never any doubt about who reigned – there were seven board members chaired by Hugh Cunningham, Mary Handley was President of the fifteen-strong Friends, The Company 1978 had 21 singers and another five came under the Schools Company. Seven names appear under Administrative Staff, another thirteen for Production Staff, and the Music Staff consisted of Assistant Conductor Kim Mooney, Repetiteur David McSkimming and Chorus Master Jon Draper – a total of 39 on the payroll and another 22 off. Little wonder that the company was enjoying an increasingly high standing, both within and outside SA.

State Opera was well aware that Puccini's *La Rondine* was unlikely to attract large audiences on its own account – as one patron explained after seeing it 'Of course it's not well known – it doesn't have any famous tunes' – but the company hoped that casting Australia's favourite soprano June Bronhill in the lead would overcome any reluctance to try something new. Tenors Robin Donald, son of Australia's favourite tenor Donald Smith, and Thomas Edmonds, a hero to local audiences, could also be expected to appeal to large numbers of people, and so it proved.

James Renfrey (*News*, 24 August) thought it 'was worth a permanent place in any company's repertoire and State Opera's presentation was strikingly effective'. Conductor turned reviewer Brian Chatterton (*Australian*, 28 August) was critical of the 'serious structural uncertainties' in the work, noting that these 'give rise to some tedious patches', but awarded the orchestra 'top line artistic honours.' However Ralph Middenway (*Advertiser*, 24 August) found it wanting. 'One could argue the company has no business wasting its time and everyone's money with such a piece.' His praise for June Bronhill was unstinting. 'The lady is a skilled and very proficient professional … who can teach the others a thing or three when it comes to holding the attention, without undue fuss.' He concluded with: 'The production, visually, musically and in every other way, was highly competent. But Gawd, it's a tedious piece.'

The general manager's introduction in the *Figaro* program referred to the decision by the Music Board of the Australia Council to reduce funding to the regional opera companies and gradually to withdraw them completely, leaving each state government to take care of its own backyard. This decision was especially galling, coming just at the time when demand for their services was increasing as never before, especially in South Australia. Campbell also wrote of The Opera Conference, a new body set up by the executive heads of the national and six state companies to assist each other to withstand the pressures of decreasing funding.

The announcement in November 1978 of the following year's joint season with The Australian Opera brought some caustic comments about the repertoire. From the national company, *Madama Butterfly*, *The Merry Widow* and *The Queen of Spades*—from the local one *The Secret Marriage*, *Werther*, *The Elixir of Love*, *One Man Show* and a gala season of *Die Fledermaus* to celebrate the opening of the refurbished and renamed Opera Theatre. Many of the country's best singers (Joan Sutherland, Joan Carden, Marilyn Richardson, Gerald English), directors and designers (Lotfi Mansouri, Colin George, John Copley, Anthony Besch, John Stoddart) and conductors (Richard Bonynge, Myer Fredman) were listed in a program stretching from March to November. A conservative collection on the whole, but the time for complaining that State Opera had 'gone grand' was well and truly over. And after all, Tchaikovsky's *Queen of Spades* and Massenet's *Werther* were rarely performed, and Nicholas Maw's *One Man Show* was little over a decade old. Some reservations were expressed about seeing Joan Sutherland, making her first appearance in Adelaide since 1965, as the very merry widow Hanna Glawari. Ralph Middenway (*Advertiser*, 3 November) likened this casting to 'using a Cadillac limousine when what is needed is an Alpha convertible', but others who had seen Australia's favourite singer in flighty roles knew that she had a wonderful natural comic gift and relished the prospect.

SOSA continued to expand the range of its activities in 1979. Accusations that Ian Campbell's aim was to create another Australian Opera in Adelaide were somewhat exaggerated, but there was no doubt that his years as a singer with the national company and his stint with the Australia Council as project officer with special responsibility for opera had underpinned his natural instinct for operating on a large scale. Not for him the limitations of state or other territorial boundaries. Driven by enlightened self-interest, he was well aware that whatever was good for State Opera was good for him.

Touring within South Australia had been common practice since the era of Intimate Opera Group and had continued under the new régime. Taking productions to the other states was the best way of demonstrating just how successful and productive SOSA had become. A return visit to the Perth Festival in February with *Marriage of Figaro* confirmed the success of a previous visit two years earlier, and in May *The Secret Marriage* went to Hobart. Apart from the political benefits accruing from these enterprises, there was the added incentive of taking advantage of Myer Fredman's extensive touring experience with the Glyndebourne productions.

Significant as these events were in enhancing the company's reputation abroad, the re-opening in March of The Opera Theatre after six months of renovations was a milestone not only for State Opera but also for Adelaide. The original Tivoli Theatre, built in 1913, held 3,000 in stalls, circle and gallery – known as the gods of course – and was said to have the largest stage in the southern hemisphere. Named variously the Prince of Wales (for a royal visit in 1917) and later Her Majesty's after being renovated by J.C. Williamson, it changed again to The Opera Theatre when bought by the State Government in 1977. The latest refurbishments were designed to restore the opulence of the 1920s, with a colour scheme of black, grey, burgundy and gold. Lots of gold. Capacity was reduced to just over 1,000 comfortable seats, the acoustics improved and inaudible air-conditioning added. Major alterations to the foyer included elegant staircases to twin bars on the first floor, and a spectacular chandelier, consisting of thousands of tiny glass tubes arranged in three tiers and weighing more than 300 kilograms. It hung in front of the stage, to be winched up into the ceiling before performances began – intentionally or not, it encouraged patrons to be seated early in order to watch this amazing sight – something akin to the Wurlitzer that sank into the floor at the Regent theatre before the movie began.

The grand opening of The Opera Theatre with a gala performance of *Die Fledermaus* on 10 March was nothing short of brilliant. Celebrations began in the Central Market across the road in Grote Street, where 1,000 invited evening-dressed guests, including many state luminaries, the Governor of South Australia Keith Seaman and the famous soprano Joan Hammond, plus a number of the sponsors who had made it all possible, were primed for a sparkling night with sparkling wine. Preceding the opera came speeches by

Hugh Cunningham and the Premier, Des Corcoran, standing in for Don Dunstan who was attending but still too frail to perform the ceremony. His role in the processes that led to this wonderful occasion was acknowledged with the unveiling of a plaque in the foyer proclaiming

This theatre was opened as
The Opera Theatre
by the Hon. Don Dunstan Q.C., M.P.
Premier of South Australia
on March 10, 1979

Not strictly correct, perhaps, but in the right spirit.

Praise for both The Opera Theatre and the opera that celebrated its opening flowed as freely as the before-and-after champagne, and using the Central Market as the dining room invited designations of SOSA as 'the Covent Garden of the South'. Coverage of the event from interstate was generous and mainly approving. Major dissension was expressed by Peter Ward (*Australian*, 4 April). With characteristic acerbity, he described the new treasure as 'a kind of high budget, low-brow-municipal-tarted-up-kitsch', but also allowed 'a big E for effort ... for overall functional improvements and efficiency'. His tirade concluded with a challenge. 'What right has Adelaide's cultural mafiosi to their cultural pretensions, when they allow such dismal lapses in public taste to occur?' Maybe the designers had overdone the glitter, but the many thousands who have enjoyed operas, plays, dance, musicals and all manner of spectacles since 1979 simply did not care. Possibly they did not even notice. Certainly at the opening, the excitement of the new surroundings, the incongruity of tramping around the fruit and vegetable stalls in full evening regalia for drinks and supper focussed everyone on having a jolly good time. The irrepressible Shirley Despoja captured the flavour (*Advertiser*, 12 March). 'The market was a bit like a kid's dream of paradise – a big rock candy mountain; brightly lit fruit stalls from which you could help yourself; hot dogs, pies and sweetmeats for the asking; chestnuts, flowers and balloons pressed into guests' hands; buskers and even a Pearly King. Champagne overflowed the plastic glasses and people licked their dripping fingers. Sauce spurted from hot dogs and people laughed and mopped their finery.'

1979 also brought a number of initiatives that were, at least in part, forced on the company for financial reasons. From the time when New Opera South Australia was incorporated, subsidies had come from both the state (an initial grant in 1973 of $15,000) and federal governments. During the 1970s the Music Board of the Australia Council (and many of its non-opera clients) had become increasingly concerned at the large proportion of its funds being consumed by opera, the largest share naturally going to The Australian Opera and the rest parcelled out between the regional companies in Perth, Brisbane, Adelaide and Melbourne. By 1979 the Board, arguing that state companies should be properly supported by their own state governments, gave advance notice that federal funding to the regionals would cease in mid 1981.

What had begun as philanthropy now became an urgent necessity. From as early as 1975, SOSA's annual reports and programs show increasing numbers of companies, businesses and individuals contributing to the company's coffers. Hugh Cunningham, chairman of NOSA and SOSA from 1974 to 1981, sang tenor in the chorus of many productions from 1972 and assisted in the founding of the Corinthian Singers in 1963. An accountant with Elders Lensworth Finance Ltd, he knew of his chief executive's interest in opera, and enlisted his company's support by placing paid advertisements in programs in 1975. By 1980 donations from patrons amounted to $20,950. In that same year the Australia Council's support was $56,000. When the latter was phased out completely, pressure grew on SOSA to increase the former. Seeing the need to pursue private support with more vigour, and encouraged by gift of $100 from American newcomer Lillian Scott to show her appreciation of *Die Fledermaus*, the company launched a Patrons Program in April 1979, inviting supporters to join at one of three levels ranging from $50 to $500. Advertiser Newspapers Limited, a major contributor to the opening of The Opera Theatre, headed the first published list of donors. By 1998 private sector support had increased greatly, and twenty-eight separate companies, among them some of the state's largest and most prominent, were acknowledged in the annual report, along with hundreds of organisations and individuals donating amounts from $100 to $15,000. This fact alone is an indication of the confidence and respect State Opera commanded from its own community and further afield. Two of its supporters, advertising agency Ogilvy and Mather and builder

A.W. Baulderstone received national Business in the Arts Awards in 1978 and 1979.

But not all sides of Parliament were equally approving. From 1972, when negotiations were in train between the main players of Intimate Opera Group and senior arts executives in the government, through the establishment of the professional New Opera SA, to State Opera's status as a statutory authority in 1976 and thereafter, relations with the government had been on the whole extremely cordial. That there were dissenters was demonstrated unequivocally on 5 March 1978 when *Hansard* reports that Leader of the Australian Democrats in the House of Assembly, Robin Millhouse, mounted an attack on the Premier via State Opera.

The member for Mitcham issued a litany of accusations and complaints, among them being that the Government could not afford SOSA's current subsidy of $585,000, that its 'patronage was a good deal lower than ... the State Theatre Company' ('It is not,' interjected Premier Dunstan), that it is 'apparently aiming to be a second national company' and that 'it does not use South Australian artists and almost all of the artists are imported from other states.' In a ludicrous and inaccurate finale Millhouse claimed to have heard that 'Mr Cunningham, the Director, is an absolute dictator and tells the artists and everyone else just what they have to do, and there is much discontent'. Hugh Cunningham was the Chairman of the Board – there was no position of Director – and was held not only in great esteem but also genuinely liked by everyone in the company from general manager to tea-lady. Although Millhouse did not name his sources, he did refer by name to a number of local singers who 'are not being used by State Opera'. The backstage cat could well have been the conduit. The Leader of the Opposition, David Tonkin, took up the argument, alluding to 'projects dear to the Premier's heart' receiving state funds while others did not. Through it all apart from his one reply, the premier, who also was responsible for the arts, kept mum. Others did not.

Ian Campbell refused to comment on the Democrat leader's claims, but declared that while funds for the company would increase by only 15 per cent in 1979 performances would be up by 106 per cent, with roughly double the previous year's output, and that average attendances had gone from 3,000 in 1976 to 6,500 in 1978. Ralph Middenway (*Advertiser*, 12 October) took up the challenge, giving facts and figures about performances for city and country audiences, for school children and young people. After the 1977/78 annual report was published, Shirley Despoja joined the fray (*Advertiser*, 30 January 1979) with reminders of the special programs, concerts and lectures offered to the public in addition to their productions, and pointing out that five of the six in the period under review had sold more than 90 per cent of available seats.

A repeat season of *The Secret Marriage* in May marked the last production for State Opera by Adrian Slack. Ian Campbell acknowledged his work in the program. 'Adrian has provided a valuable service to the company in its most important formative years and I am sure that all of our audiences will join me in wishing him much success in his developing career in the United Kingdom.' On the eve of his departure to become Director of Productions for Welsh National Opera and Artistic Director of the Wexford Festival in Eire, Slack was interviewed by John Kirby (*Mail*, 29 May) and acknowledged the value of his three years in Adelaide. 'I was bloody lucky to get a job like this. I've been able to grow a lot.' Seeing Adelaide as 'a fairly quiet corner of the world' he found 'it was an opportunity to fall flat on my face without disgracing myself'. He may not have distinguished himself here, but he did not disgrace himself either (except in suggesting that Adelaide was not the cultural capital of the world and that failure here was of no consequence).

But his departure had considerable consequences for the triumvirate. Slack had been appointed by Campbell's predecessor and was the choice of Myer Fredman on the strength of their Glyndbourne associations. Campbell's reasons for not persuading Slack to renew his contract can only be guessed at, but his departure fitted nicely with the former's plans to engage a range of directors of his choice to suit each production – an argument with much merit.

State Opera and its predecessor New Opera had built up an impressive record of taking productions to schools, working on a common but unproven premise that thus were the audiences of the future assured. In some cases bookings in conjunction with the Arts Council of South Australia enabled the company to keep a small number of singers in full-time employment for up to a year, and at times a Schools Company was separately listed. Some of the pieces were commissioned – *Parrot Pie* by Peter Tahourdin, *Sid the Serpent Who Wanted to Sing* by Malcolm Fox (the most successful of them all), Peter

Narroway's *Ticka-Tocka-Linga* and Jeff Carroll's *Professor Kobalt and the Krimson Kokonut*. Many of these gave children the opportunity to participate, a practice with the added advantage of helping to maintain order.

Beginning in 1977, through the initiative of Schools Officer Victoria Owens, a Study Guide was produced each season with information presented in straightforward, non-jargonistic language about each of the forthcoming operas. The material was aimed at secondary school level, but also proved extremely valuable for tertiary students.

A joint venture with the Music Branch of the Education Department through the good offices of Alan Farwell (he was also responsible for the appointment of a School's Officer on secondment from the ED) took the next step, moving from participation pieces to introducing young people to proper opera by allowing them to perform in full-scale productions to paying audiences. The first of what became common practice for the following eight years, Britten's *Let's Make an Opera* gave twelve children the chance to share the stage with five professional singers, to be accompanied by a small orchestra, to come under the professional baton of Myer Fredman and the direction of experienced singer Kevin Miller, and to learn what a thrilling reward can be theirs in return for a lot of hard work and acceptance of strict discipline.

By the time of the next production, Donizetti's rollicking comedy about quackery *The Elixir of Love,* Jon Draper had taken a step nearer his goal by moving from Chorus Master to Assistant Conductor, and took over from Fredman for two of the performances. And Ian Campbell fulfilled one of his ambitions by engaging as director Colin George, Artistic Director of the State Theatre Company, for his swansong to South Australia. Jim Coogan, manager of the company's workshop, was also given the chance of a lifetime. He designed and built a dreadfully, beautifully kitsch electric car for Dulcamara to cart himself and his supplies of the magic potion (actually cheap Bordeaux) around the villages. A scene stealer, this, far more effective than children and dogs. *Opera Australia* editor David Gyger made a special trip to Adelaide for this occasion, and praised (August 1979) George for finding levels of subtlety usually submerged under the 'froth and bubble' of the piece. Gyger liked the cast – Roger Howell, Carolyn Vaughan, Patsy Hemingway, Thomas Edmonds and James Christiansen, and was especially impressed that the last two had been 'liberated from the dramatic sameness' of previous sightings. Peter Ward (*Australian*, 11 July) repeated his scathing criticisms of the new Opera Theatre and its 'execrable chocolate box interior', dismissing the Donizetti as 'a musical confection that hasn't the least trace of a hard centre'.

Nicholas Maw's *One Man Show*, a satire on the pretensions and posings of the world of visual art – it is about painters and art critics, but offers plenty of parallels to the world of music – attracted enormous interest around the country. Sydney's Professor Donald Peart wrote it up in *Opera Australia*'s featured centre spread in September, and in the pre-publicity period photographs appeared all over town of Gerald English standing on his head and singing the role of British State Gallery Director Sir Horace Stringfellow – the sudden rush of blood is supposed to clear up his problems. Ian Campbell claimed two firsts – the ABC broadcast the performance on 15 September live on national radio, and the show was taken to the Sydney Opera House for three performances in October and included in The Australian Opera's subscription

Dulcamara's Cart, *The Elixir of Love*, 1979

series. His announcement of this coup contained both a compliment for State Opera and a dig at his rival, Victoria State Opera, which would also appear in Sydney – after State Opera.

The reviews reflected the unusual interest in the piece. All the music critics were pleased, even pernickety Peter Ward, but art expert David Dolan's 'Pot Calls the Kettle Black' (*Advertiser*, 5 September) found it lacking as 'a satire on the art world' and surmised that the main characters 'would be suspicious of anyone – critic or whoever – who was moved to rapture by so slim a plot and such relentlessly tuneless music'. Audiences for Maw were down by 10 per cent from the previous Donizetti, which was 75 per cent of capacity, but given that the English composer was virtually unknown, and even worse, still alive (not recommended for opera goers suspicious of the unknown – except at Festival time) the figures could have been much worse. In Sydney *One Man Show* recorded 77 percent of capacity. Murray Hill, SA's first Minister for the Arts, made a special trip to see his team create the precedent of being the first regional company to appear in the Sydney Opera House, and Maria Prerauer, doyen of Australia's opera critics, gave it a glowing review (*Australian*, 15 October). To the glee of some and the chagrin of others, she bluntly pronounced that 'the musical side of proceedings' steered by Myer Fredman was 'as good as and sometimes a lot better than some recent Australian Opera performances'. Balm also to the soul of Fredman, who had already decided not to renew his contract when it ran out at the end of 1980.

Massenet's *Werther*, the last mainstage production for the year, fared little better than *One Man Show*, falling six points below the 73 per cent average for the year. Jim Coogan was again in the promotional news, this time for building exact replicas of the toys that the child Hans would have played with in 1820, including a handmade rocking horse with a mane of silk. Directed and designed by Anthony Besch and John Stoddart, whose partnership had been greatly admired in the *Così fan tutte* of 1975, and with Stephen Haas, the romantic lead from *Die Fledermaus* and imported Scottish soprano Cynthia Buchan as the doomed lovers Werther and Charlotte, this story of unrequited love pleased the critics. James Renfrey (*News*, 31 October) argued that 'one reason for its big success is that both conductor and director don't hesitate to pull out all the stops, including the tremolo, so to say', and David Gyger (*Opera*

Australia, December 1979) judged it a 'considerable success, coming close to an ideal stage realisation of the work for our times'.

What a year was 1979 for SOSA. Five productions, interstate tours to Perth, Hobart and Sydney and others within SA for both adult and school audiences, formation of a purpose-built orchestra, the introduction of a Patrons Program, a refurbished theatre all of its own, the departure (and non-replacement) of the Director of Productions, new appointments of an Assistant Conductor and a Co-ordinator of the In Sight program for schools and news that from 1981 there would be a new Musical Director. Even better, these events were being reported regularly in newspapers and journals around Australia and overseas – State Opera of South Australia was firmly inked in on the world's operatic map.

And there was not much of a break over Christmas because the 1980 Adelaide Festival of Arts, and a brand new production of Britten's *Death in Venice*, was just around the corner.

9

Musical Chairs – 1980–84

✣

Myer Fredman's decision not to renew his contract as Musical Director of State Opera was publicly announced in October 1979. Asked for reasons, he said that having held the position for six years he felt the need to move on, and to resume the international career he had relinquished to come to Australia. The *Advertiser*, (25 October) reported that: 'Mr Fredman would not say whether non-renewal of his contract was because of dissatisfaction within the company. He said that his contract prevented him from making any criticism of the company.' The chairman of State Opera, Hugh Cunningham, was quoted in the same report as paying tribute to Fredman's work, saying that a large part of the credit for the company's progress over the past five years was due to him.

The common view on this matter was that relations between Fredman and the general manager had begun to turn sour. In interviews with Alan Hodgson in 1982, after Campbell decided that he too was ready to move on, he acknowledged that during 1979 he was aware of some resentment growing over a perception that he had become the public face of the company, leaving Fredman in the shadow. When the matter was brought to the attention of the Board, several attempts were made to resolve the problem, and offers were made of a new, more flexible contract. But Fredman's mind was obviously made up, and his decision to leave eventually had to be accepted.

Conflicts and tussles for power between general managers and musical directors are part and parcel of the lives of opera companies. It is interesting to note that while SOSA was experiencing its first taste of offstage prima donnas jostling for pole position the same struggle was going on in the national company. Musical Director Richard Bonynge and General Manager Peter Hemmings were at loggerheads over repertoire and casting, one of the major sticking points being Hemmings's wish to cast Joan Sutherland as the monarch in Britten's *Gloriana*, a suggestion which the great soprano's husband, also her sole conductor, found outrageous. The Australian Opera Board of Directors was initially split equally between the two. After many meetings of deadly earnestness – only in hindsight did the pictures of the two protagonists entering and leaving the boardroom separately and by different doors become ludicrous – all but one of the Directors gradually lined up in support of the Musical Director. Peter Hemmings returned to England as General Manager of the 1980 Edinburgh Festival, and his distinguished career in arts administration led him eventually in 1984 to become General Director of Los Angeles Opera until his retirement in 2000.

In Adelaide the pendulum swung the other way. In both places however the productions kept coming, filling the stages of the Sydney Opera House and the Adelaide Festival and Opera Theatres and never showing the slightest sign of the tumult and lobbying raging behind the scenes.

The difference of opinion over casting at The Australian Opera was duplicated in Adelaide over the choice of a tenor to play Aschenbach, the tortured soul at the core of Britten's *Death in Venice*. The General Manager was trespassing on Fredman's territory by insisting on Australian veteran Robert Gard, but the choice was handsomely vindicated by performances that conveyed with physically painful realism the anguish of an aging man over his obsessional infatuation with a young Adonis, and led to an invitation to act, and eventually also to sing, the role in a privately made film of the opera.

Besides being the Australian première, SOSA's *Death in Venice* attracted an unusual amount of pre-publicity from sources well outside the usual. The Peter Stuyvesant Cultural Foundation gave a sponsorship of $30,000, designer

Luciana Arrighi was the subject of articles from visual arts writers, and the Archbishop of Adelaide published an article on homosexuality. Lance Campbell (*Advertiser*, 15 March) wrote most movingly of Robert Gard's dedication to his role and his determination to fulfil the expectations of his wife that he would excel in it, dealing courageously with her death from cancer during the rehearsal period. With Gard in the leading role, a large number of respected singers (Tom McDonnell, Roger Howell, Anthony Bremner) in the cameo parts, the boy Tadzio (dancer Ian Wilkinson) and the gracious, aloof Basia Bonkowski as his mother, both establishing their characters through movement alone, with Arrighi's perfect period costumes, Brian

Robert Gard, Tom McDonnell,
Death in Venice, 1980

Thomson's simple stylised set and Jim Sharman's apparently effortless direction, with Myer Fredman and the pick of the Adelaide Symphony Orchestra in the pit, the ingredients were undeniably the best collection SOSA, and arguably any other regional opera company in Australia, had ever assembled.

One small setback resulted in a rare treat for a favoured few. A special preview had to be cancelled because Tom McDonnell was stricken with a throat infection. Rather than waste a rehearsal opportunity, director Jim Sharman walked through the seven cameo roles himself while Jon Draper sang them from a music stand stage left. 'Myer, I'm a tenor, not a baritone,' he protested rather feebly when appointed to the task with less than twelve hours' notice – but he got on with it anyway. Truly a night to remember for the small invited audience, and a salutory reminder of the extraordinary skills demanded of all concerned.

No wonder the critics were scrambling for superlatives. Since *Midsummer Marriage* in 1978, interstate papers had been sending their writers to cover the Adelaide Festivals, a major draw being the Australian premières of important contemporary operas. Readers of the Melbourne *Age*, the *Bulletin, Sydney Morning Herald* and *Opera Australia* from Sydney, the national daily, the *Australian,* and *Opera* magazine in London learnt that with *Death in Venice* Adelaide had brought off a triumph on all counts. To ensure that subscribers were also properly informed of the company's achievement the program of the next production carried a selection of quotes from interstate publications – 'Stunning Australian première'; 'the most fertile, alluring and eloquent production yet accorded an Adelaide festival opera'; a 'supreme achievement in the production of opera in this century'.

During the planning stages of *Death in Venice* references were made to the possibility of transferring the production to Sydney – Robert Gard was after all one of The Australian Opera's most admired principal artists – and several writers made mention of this likelihood. Within TAO there was considerable interest, and some enthusiasm, but not quite enough. Sydney had to wait until 1989 to see this outstanding music drama, re-created by the original team from Adelaide. And Robert Gard was at last able to play what many have seen as his most challenging and most rewarding role for his own company in his own city.

Just about anything would have been an anticlimax after Britten's masterpiece. Francesco Cavalli had a resounding success in 1644 with *L'Ormindo,* a typical baroque tale of romance, intrigue and murder in the courts of Morocco in the sixteenth century. Doubtless encouraged by its success with Monteverdi's *The Coronation of Poppea* in 1977, State Opera engaged Anthony Besch and John Stoddart to direct and design for Cavalli and brought tenor Graeme Wall to sing the princely title role. It worked for Warren Bourne (*Advertiser,* 2 May) but not even William Bamford decked out in a long dress to hide his hairy legs in the comic drag role of Erice could convince David Gyger (*Opera Australia* June 1980). James Renfrey (*News,* 5 May) admitted that he 'hopped it after five scenes, considering that a fair hearing'. The glitzy surroundings of the 1920s (*pace* Peter Ward) Opera Theatre did not help to transport the audience to sixteenth-century Morocco, whereas the simplicity of the Playhouse had readily adapted itself to Nero's court for *Poppea*.

A new production of Donizetti's *Don Pasquale* settled the dust raised by *L'Ormindo*, though some small clouds accompanied director and designer Tom Lingwood, who had just severed his connections with TAO after 13 years over irreconcilable artistic differences. His work for State Opera was especially admired because he managed to create a setting that worked both in the Opera Theatre and in the country towns where the production later toured. Grant Dickson was the bumbling, vain, aged Don, Judith Henley the manipu-

lating minx who weds him only so she can wangle a decent inheritance for her true love, and Thomas Edmonds the winner of her heart and his uncle's fortune.

Their machinations were nicely encapsulated in a cartoon reproduced in the program showing Donizetti composing an *opera seria* with his left hand and an *opera buffa* with his right. The touring cast, with Keith Hempton as the Don and William Bamford as his naughty nephew had two city performances, with Jon Draper conducting, before embarking on their Arts Council-sponsored visits to nine country centres, spread out from Mount Gambier to Port Lincoln, over two weeks.

In addition to producing information brochures for school students for each production, Wendy Mead, Director of the aptly named In Sight youth program, collaborated with the staff and students of the Adelaide College of Arts and

1840 caricature of Donizetti, writing an *opera seria* with his left hand and an *opera buffa* with his right.

Education to put on abridgements of *Così fan tutte* in May and *Don Pasquale* in July for school audiences. Using State Opera sets and costumes, directed by

Kevin Miller and conducted by Brian Chatterton, these scaled-down versions allowed over 4,000 young people a real sample of opera, as well as giving aspiring singers and players opportunities to display their wares to live audiences.

Franz Lehár's *The Land of Smiles* was offered in September as State Opera's share of a joint operetta (*sic*) season with The Australian Opera's *Patience*. A strong cast was led by Thomas Edmonds, Judith Henley, William Bamford and Heather Ross, and Anthony Besch was once more called in to direct, this time with Peter Cooke as designer. By a stroke of sheer luck Viennese-born and -bred Henry Krips (brother of the more famous Josef) was living in Adelaide, where he was Conductor-in-Chief for the Adelaide Symphony Orchestra. His connections with Lehár included having met the composer on many occasions and conducting his opera *Giuditta* in his presence in 1937 with renowned tenor Richard Tauber. Whatever other criticisms were levelled at Krips, there was no argument that he knew his Viennese repertoire and was the best person around to conduct *The Land of Smiles*. High expectations were held also for Adelaide's tenor lead. A few days before the opening, Jim Robbins (*Advertiser*, 4 September) described Thomas Edmonds as 'a man who is loved in SA as much for himself as for his singing' in a laudatory article accompanied by a priceless photograph of Our Tom decked out in tutu, tights and tiara for *No One Loves a Fairy When She's Forty*. Most reviews praised Krips's sense of style, one referring to his 'authentic baton', and approved Peter Cooke's designs while finding the piece dated. David Gyger (*Opera Australia*, October 1980) concluded that the work is 'worth an occasional airing despite its flaws' and that this production 'in general emphasised its strengths and swept most of its weaknesses under the carpet'. Tristram Cary (*Sunday Mail*, 14 September) was less charitable, coupling Lehár with Cavalli in his accusation that State Opera was 'lavishing much time and effort on works that are not of the first rank'. Peter Cooke's 'beautiful sets and costumes ... saved the evening from utter banality', except for 'Edmonds's last act headdress' which 'reminded me of Tenniel's loonier illustrations for Alice'. Cary differed from most other writers in his assessment of the music. 'In the pit ... Henry Krips did his best to get the Boskowsky delivery, but it didn't quite happen.' The reference to the famed Willi, legendary for the lilt in his baton, identifies Cary's measuring stick.

Costume designs by Kenneth Rowell, *The Tales of Hoffmann*, 1982

Above: Chorus, *Falstaff*, 1982

Left: Men's chorus, *The Pearl Fishers*, 1983

Top: Women's chorus, *The Pearl Fishers*, 1983
Above: Members of the Court, *Rigoletto*, 1985

Costume design by Ken Wilby and Mark Thompson,
Sweeney Todd, 1987

Top: Yvonne Minton, *Elektra*, 1991
Above: Marilyn Zschau, *Elektra*, 1991

Top: John Pringle, Jordan Welden-Iley and Yoko Wantanabe, *Madama Butterfly*, 1991

Left: Men's chorus, *Carmen*, 1993

Top: Women's chorus, *Carmen*, 1993
Above left: Yoko Watanabe, *Adriana Lecouvreur*, 1994
Above right: Malcolm Donnelly, *Falstaff*, 1995

❧

This page and opposite: Men's chorus, changing civvies for uniforms, *Il trovatore*, 1999

Prudence Dunstone, *The Mikado*, 1999

Top: Wendy Hopkins, Timothy Sexton, Brian Gilbertson and Carolyn Ferrie,
Sid the Serpent, 1998
Above: Anke Höppner, *Madama Butterfly*, 1999

✆

Top: Daniel Sumeji, Stuart Skelton and Deborah Riedel, *Tosca*, 2000
Above: Deborah Riedel and Stuart Skelton, *Tosca*, 2000

Top: Malcolm Donnelly, Peter Keller and John Wegner, *Das Rheingold*, 1998
Above: Elizabeth Campbell and John Wegner, *Das Rheingold*, 1998

Top: Liane Keegan,
Siegfried, 1998

Left: Edward Cook,
Siegfried, 1998

Top: Cast of *Nixon in China* at dinner, 1992.
Clockwise from left: James Maddalena, David Porcelijn, Dawn Wallace, Geoffrey Harris,
Shelley Hayton, Greg Roberts, Vanessa Berger, Mark McSweeney and Bill Gillespie.
Above: John Tuckey, Dawn Wallace and Christopher Stone, Introduction to *La Bohème*,
Enterprise House, 1995

❦

Left: Diana Ramsay, AO
and Maureen Mowbray,
mid-year Christmas luncheon,
Radisson Playford, 2000

Below: Lady Neal and
Jeanette Sandford-Morgan,
launch of Season 2000,
Adelaide Festival Theatre

The contrast between Lehár and Tchaikovsky, between the concocted trivialities of high life in Vienna and Peking in *The Land of Smiles* and the totally credible, quintessentially Russian realism of *Eugene Onegin* could not have been greater. And there could not have been a more appropriate swansong for Myer Fredman, about to depart to take up his new position as Head of the Opera and Vocal Department at the State Conservatorium of New South Wales. The lush romanticism built in to the instrumental and vocal lines of the score suited his style, giving his innate emotionalism full reign. His departure and his services to State Opera were generously acknowledged in the reviews, and the program carried two pages of action pictures and a selection of accolades from local and national publications for his musical direction over the previous six years. Over the page from 'Farewell to Musical Director Myer Fredman' was 'Welcome to Musical Director Denis Vaughan'. Not, perhaps, the most sensitive juxtaposition.

Onegin also marked the end of Jon Draper's association with SOSA. He had a special gift with the chorus, getting them to sing with great verve and projection without shouting. Their work-to-rule fruit-picking would not have earned them any socialist medals, but their tone, ensemble and precision would.

The message 'From the General Manager' in the *Onegin* program included the news that from 1981 State Opera and TAO would present separate seasons, subscribers having indicated this as their preference. Loyalty to the local company had turned out to be of prime importance.

In August 1980 State Opera had sent a deputation of chairman Hugh Cunningham and general manager Ian D. Campbell to interview Denis Vaughan, subsequently confirmed as the favoured candidate chosen from around 50 applicants for Fredman's replacement. Born in Melbourne in 1926, Vaughan had established an impressive record in England and Europe as a keyboard player and conductor, as well as writing scholarly texts on a number of composers, on acoustics and on authenticity in performance. At the time of his appointment he was on the music staff of the State Opera of Bavaria in Munich. His appointment as Musical Director of State Opera for a term of three years from January 1981 was announced on 5 September, 1980.

On his arrival, the new appointee was interviewed by Angela Bevin (*Advertiser*, 28 January). He expressed the hope that he could 'boost the demand for opera in Adelaide so it can eventually become a nightly event'. Totally unrealistic, of course, but praiseworthy for its idealism. A few weeks later, Ian Campbell announced that he had withdrawn from negotiations with Scottish Opera over their general manager position and would remain to fulfil his contract in Adelaide.

A handsome brochure for the 1981 season advertised the upcoming operas and included a précis of each plot and photographs of the general manager, musical director and all performers. *La Bohème* and *HMS Pinafore* had both been staged by SOSA within the previous four years, and this time around Marilyn Richardson promised an outstanding Mimi and Dennis Olsen, a great favourite in Adelaide for his marvellous comic gifts (not to mention his uniquely funny knees) was to direct the G and S and also play Sir Joseph Porter KGB in a new production. *Carmen* and *The Barber of Seville*, both well up on the list of operas patrons most wanted to see, were new for the company, as was *A Christmas Carol*, Scottish-born composer Thea Musgrave's setting of the Dickens classic. State Opera was obviously playing it safe, a wise policy in the light of the $291,495 deficit accrued from the previous financial year. Most of the singers were already familiar, a new voice being Australian mezzo-soprano Rachel Gettler, then working at Mannheim Opera, cast in the crucial role of Carmen. Directors of considerable repute new to the company had been engaged – Robin Lovejoy from the Australian Elizabethan Theatre Trust, American Tito Capobianco, already known in Australia for his productions with Joan Sutherland, and Ian Campbell would be taking the director's baton out of his manager's briefcase to put himself up for inspection with *La Bohème* and *Carmen*.

Denis Vaughan's debut with *Pinafore* in the Adelaide Festival Theatre in March went well. His program notes claimed the 'novelty' of being able to work from the full score, and expressed his hope that the 'rare poetry' of Sullivan's music would be 'recaptured'. Thus primed, two of Adelaide's most widely read critics quoted him and found that his aims had been achieved. In addition to pulling in full houses, *Pinafore* was recorded by the ABC for simulcast on ABC television and FM radio on 11 October, the first time that a regional opera company had been recognised in this way and of great credit both to State Opera and to Campbell's enterprise. The ABC does not enter into such agreements merely out of the goodness of its heart.

After eight years of board stability, State Opera was about to see three chairmen come and go in the next three years. The first of these, appointed in March 1981 by the Minister of Arts Murray Hill, was Kevin Miller, an Adelaide tenor who had recently returned to Adelaide after working in England for 25 years and was running opera and vocal studies at the Adelaide College of Arts and Education. Hugh Cunningham, the first treasurer of New Opera and Chairman since 1974, was appointed as a member of the board for a further three years. Probably in principle it was time for a change, but Cunningham was so effective, well respected and liked that practice could have overcome principle. The letters and cards that were showered on him at his retirement were testament in abundance, and Justin Macdonnell has saluted him as 'the best chairman I ever had, and I wish that anyone who ever managed an arts company would be as fortunate as I was'.

Similar turnover in general managers was also in the offing, but for the next eighteen months Ian Campbell was staying put.

Chorus scene, *HMS Pinafore*, 1981

In March the In Sight program collaborated with the Music Branch of the Education Department and the Centre for the Performing Arts to form the State Opera Youth Company, which made its debut with seven performances of Richard Rodney Bennett's *All the King's Men* during the 1981 Come Out Festival for young people. Students from thirty-three primary, secondary and private schools were involved in singing and playing this version of the seventeenth-century battle between Royalists and Roundheads that Humpty Dumpty enshrined in children's folk lore. Dean Patterson conducted and Brian Debnam, from the Stage Company, was the director.

Another link with New Opera was broken – or rather stretched – in May when planning manager Russell Mitchell, whose association dates back to his backstage work as a drama student on the IOG season in 1972 at Flinders University, left Adelaide to take up a similar position with The Australian Opera.

Each of the remaining four productions for 1981 was commendable in some special aspect, giving the company its best year so far. *La Bohème* found general favour for Ian Campbell's direction within Tom Lingwood's TAO sets, for Marilyn Richardson's fragile and tender Mimi and for Vaughan's detailed conducting, though the effect of returning to Puccini's original intentions was rather less dramatic than he had hoped. 6,200 Opera Theatre seats were sold, and subscriptions rose to 4,011. Giving the public what they wanted was obviously a good formula. *Carmen* did even better – Bizet's greatest hits sold out four weeks before the opening. Not surprisingly, experienced journalists (as distinct from opera critics) Peter Ward and Lance Campbell were both greatly taken with the charismatic Argentinian director Tito Capobianco, writing eminently readable interviews about him and his enduring affair with Carmen. In the event his seventh attempt to capture the essence of opera's best known heroine, while largely successful and pleasing many of the critics, was foiled. Rachel Gettler sang with all the fire and passion one could wish, but Carmen's sensuality, her contempt for a discarded lover and her final abandonment to her fate did not reach her body. James Renfrey (*News*, 10 August) found her 'more cerebral than sensual and altogether too subtle and restrained'. Of all the critics, Ken Healey was least impressed by Denis Vaughan's claims (once again) of authenticity, accusing him (*Canberra Times*, 30 August) of reducing the score 'to a succession of flabby tunes, utterly without rhythmic vitality', and holding him responsible for a dampening effect on both the leads. Probably this production would have made a bigger and more effective picture in the Festival Theatre than in the Opera Theatre where it had to be played because of clashing bookings.

A straight run of successes – give or take occasional objections from the critics – was continued with a riotous *Barber*, Roger Howell earning a swag of compliments for his Figaro and Tom Lingwood being accorded much of the credit for his applaudable sets. Graeme Young from the Queensland Opera Company, appointed as assistant musical director in July to replace Jon Draper, conducted two nights of the Rossini classic.

But the best of 1981 was yet to come. When Ian Campbell attended the world première of Thea Musgrave's *A Christmas Carol* in Norfolk, Virginia in 1979 he determined to secure the first Australian performances for State Opera. His judgement was unerring. A classic Christmas story, played in late November with a stellar cast led by James Christiansen as Scrooge, Dennis Olsen as the Spirit of Christmas, Thomas Edmonds, Edwin Hodgeman, Judith Henley and Roger Howell in a whole bundle of cameo parts, Greg Cunningham (son of Hugh) as Tiny Tim and a crowd of gifted children – a grand finale to a fine year was practically guaranteed. And as the shining star on the top of the tree, the composer herself attended (by courtesy of the British Council and Myer SA Stores Ltd) the final week of rehearsals and the opening night.

During the lead-up a dissenting voice was heard. Australian composer John Terry was incensed that State Opera had chosen to present a Dickens opera by a foreign composer without even having considered his own version of the same story, called *Ebenezer*. His vexation was exacerbated by the fact that his piece had been shown in a workshop at Fremont High School, that State Opera had been invited but only one board member turned up. Sorry, said the company – we have had the Musgrave piece on our books for over two years.

The Christmas Carol was widely praised as a work – 'this is an opera to be savoured for its happiness, all the richer for the hurtfulness against which it is shown' (Ralph Middenway, *Advertiser*, 16 November); 'a contemporary opera of compelling musical interest, ingeniously contrived and beautifully presented' (James Renfrey, *News*, 16 November); 'music with the bite of winter winds,

Thomas Edwards, Greg Cunningham, Jolanta Nagajek, Judith Henley, Gina Cohen
and Andrew Muir, *A Christmas Carol*, 1981

the bitterness of poisonous murk (Romolo Costantino, *Age*, 7 December). Costantino was especially taken with James Christiansen's Scrooge, finding him 'successfully detestable' as he 'cringed and winced on the sidelines'. The whole event was most memorable in all respects, and the pre-performance picture of a group of stage waifs singing their dear little hearts out in Christmas carols outside the Opera Theatre is imprinted for ever.

'A Season of Masterpieces', the heading for the 1982 promotion, was no exaggeration. Gounod's archetypically romantic *Faust*, Offenbach's *The Tales of Hoffmann*, a sad but glorious record of a beautiful young man who kept falling in love with the wrong girls, and Verdi's last and greatest opera *Falstaff*, modelled on Shakespeare's fat, fallen hero – all undeniably major works. And a revival of the 1975 *Così fan tutte*, honoured by a National Critics Award and sought after by Scottish Opera, who borrowed John Stoddart's delicious sets and costumes for their own production in 1981. Most of the faces were familiar – by this time SOSA had a fairly stable company of about 16 on- and off-stage regulars – and new names Noel Mangin (Mephistopheles) and Kenneth Rowell (designer for *Hoffmann*) were well reputed. Soprano Gillian Sullivan was promised a warm welcome back to her home town to sing three major roles after postgraduate study and engagements in UK.

SOSA's selection of *The Makropulos Affair* by Janáček for the 1982 Adelaide Festival of Arts prompted the company's first professional manager Justin Macdonnell to record the 'immensely long and productive contribution which the Festival has made to opera in this country' (*Theatre Australia*, February 1982). Over a period of 22 years he counted up 29 Australian and six world premières, including *The Excursions of Mr Broucek* mounted by New Opera SA in 1974, the first performance of any Janáček opera in Australia.

In February, close to the opening of *Makropulos*, State Opera took delivery of the letter they had been dreading. The Australia Council confirmed that federal funding to the state opera companies would end as at 31 December 1982. With typical cheek Ian Campbell gossiped that Timothy Pascoe, the Australia Council Chairman, had adopted 'They Call me Meaney' as his theme song.

The fascination of having one of the greatest singers of our time here in Adelaide in the role of the greatest singer in the world for 300 years added immeasurably to the appeal of *Makropulos*, a fable about Emilia

Elisabeth Söderström, Roger Howell,
The Makropulos Affair, 1982

Marty, possessor of a gorgeous body, a gorgeous voice and the secret of an elixir which gives her eternal life and has preserved her at the peak of all her powers for three centuries. Swedish soprano Elisabeth Söderstrom, acclaimed for her Marty and other Janáček roles, attracted interviews with journalists from Adelaide and Melbourne, including the operatically extremely well-informed Michael Shmith (*Age*, 19 March), who was able to address her in terms of her international standing. Christabel Hirst (*Advertiser*, 24 February) wrote a woman-to-woman story, revealing that Söderstrom particularly loved Marty because she doesn't have to be good. 'As Emilia I can spit and swear and drink whisky on stage, and the role demands total involvement'. These and other articles aimed at the general public show the extent to which State Opera had become a company that belonged to everyone, not just to the cognoscenti, so everyone could be expected to take an interest in its affairs.

Engaging this distinguished soprano to sing in Adelaide was one of two major coups for SOSA. The other was getting Elijah Moshinsky, renowned for his opera and theatre productions in many of the world's most prestigious centres, to direct. In fact the two were in tandem – Söderstrom's acceptance of the job was strongly influenced by the prospect of working with Moshinsky.

They were a triumphant team. She was without question the star, sounding and looking, in Luciana Arrighi's enviable gowns and Stephen Dattner's Artic black fox furs, every inch the prima donna who had perfected the art of getting her own way, especially with men, over three centuries. To Moshinsky's great credit, she stood out only as it was appropriate against the seven men and two women, all Australians, who clearly found inspiration in sharing her stage. The sparseness of Brian Thomson's sets reflected the emptiness of her own life, and Denis Vaughan convinced the singers and the Adelaide Symphony Orchestra that Janáček was manageable, after all.

By this time the attendance of interstate critics was no longer remarkable, but, for the record, the major figures were there, and gave *Makropulos* enthusiastic and intelligently reasoned notices.

Also during the Festival, the State Opera Youth Company gave around 150 young singers and players the unforgettable excitement of performing *Noye's Fludde*, Britten's custom-built opera for a few professionals, including conductor Dean Patterson and director Brian Debnam, and many amateurs. A cute photograph of a real tiger and a stage oryx observing each other – through bars, of course – was published when some of the children visited the zoo in

Cast members try out their costumes at the Adelaide Zoo, *Advertiser*, 28 January 1982

their Casey van Sebille head-dresses in order to observe the birds and beasts at first hand. Cudgels were taken up on behalf of the SOYC when the public learned that the Education Department had decided to cease funding the salary of Wendy Mead, Co-ordinator of the In Sight program. After six months of intense lobbying which went all the way to the Premier David Tonkin, a reprieve came in the form of a grant from the Youth Performing Arts Council.

'AMBITION, SKILL, TAKE CAMPBELL TO THE MET' trumpeted the headline of Jill Sykes's announcement to Australia (*Opera Australia*, May 1982) that State Opera's general manager was not just moving on but projecting himself clear across the Pacific Ocean to the world's largest and most prominent opera company. In an extended interview with Alan Hodgson before his departure in October he discussed with characteristic frankness his time in Adelaide, his opinions about the strengths and weaknesses of his colleagues there and his relationships with the Board and with the government. Disarmingly honest also about himself, he had his eyes wide open about his prospects in New York. Starting as one of four Assistant Artistic Administrators, he set his sights firmly on the top job in that sector of the Met's operations, but he was utterly realistic that he would have to prove his worth and that nothing was guaranteed. 'Here, if I bark people listen. If I bark there I'll probably get a knife between my ribs. Here I'm a big fish in a little pond – there a little fish in a big pond.' He knew too that he would have to change. 'I like to be in charge but now I must become one of a team.'

His proposal to step down as General Manager on 2 August but remain in Adelaide to direct *Hoffmann* in September came side by side with the announcement that Larry Ruffell, administrator with Canberra Opera, would replace him.

Also in May, singers William Bamford, Jolanta Nagajek, Claire Primrose and David Brennan and director Christopher Bell, all regulars in State Opera productions, plus Rosalind Martin and pianist David McSkimming put their ambitions to the test with the first show of *The Singers' Company*. Tristram Cary (*Opera Australia*, June 1982) found that they fell short of their promises of 'new and unusual music theatre' and urged them to set their sights higher.

There was general agreement that *Faust* should have been better than it was. Director Bernd Benthaak and designer Douglas Smith had fine track records (including this production for TAO in 1971), Marilyn Richardson and Thomas Edmonds could be expected to be well on top of Faust and Marguerite, Noel Mangin's vocal and physical capacities were ideal for Mephistopheles, and the other roles were all in hands known to be capable. Perhaps the après Festival syndrome was to blame – following the triumph of *The Makropulos Affair* was going to be a tall order, and perhaps expectations were set unreasonably high. Audiences were well prepared with general interest articles by Alan Roberts on the director and Lance Campbell on the devil, and almost filled the Opera Theatre in June.

David Gyger's review (*Opera Australia*, July 1982) conveyed the most even-handed impression, deploring the over-use of explosive devices to accompany the supernatural occurrences of the first act and rightly reporting that some of them provoked laughter from the audience, but commending devices such as the scrims that took the action smoothly from place to place. Gyger was satisfied with Marguerite and Faust, but found Noel Mangin cast against his nature. James Renfrey (*News*, 7 June) agreed that 'his idea of the role seemed more hilarious than devilish'.

Given its rapturous reception in 1975, a repeat of the Besch-Stoddart *Così fan tutte* was to be expected. The director's explanation of his colour scheme's progress – 'The black and white of conventional formality into the richer colours of self-revelation and mutual understanding' – was printed this time in the program, putting his intentions beyond doubt and solving a few differences of opinion about the psychology behind it all. English tenor Robin Leggate made his Australian debut as Ferrando, and the quartet with Roger Howell, Rachel Gettler and Marilyn Richardson matched up well. James Christiansen outfoxed them all as before, this time aided and abetted by Gillian Sullivan's Despina. During rehearsals the whole cast was stricken with flu, Richardson catching up last and unable to sing the opening. To the rescue flew (literally) Lynne Cantlon, who had sung the same production in New Zealand in 1979. This *Così* was a good investment for State Opera. Its first airing was followed four years later across the Tasman, Scottish Opera took it two years later, back it came home for the second round, and Queensland Opera was after it for 1983. It's a good story to spread around when poorly informed carpers complain about money 'wasted' on 'lavish' sets and costumes. Money spent on good quality fabrics, materials and workmanship is never wasted.

Ian Campbell made his formal farewells to his audience in the *Così* program. He acknowledged the support he had enjoyed from the Board, from Myer Fredman and from both Liberal and Labor Governments, and made sure that the nuts and bolts people were recognised with 'I would like to place on record my gratitude to a dedicated and vigorous staff in all areas of the State Opera administration, workshop, wardrobe, stage management and music staff, all of whom have shown great devotion and loyalty to the State Opera of South Australia. I have been proud to be part of so talented a team'.

As Larry Ruffell moved in, Chairman Kevin Miller moved out. He was quoted as saying that 'there have been no real problems but I have agreed to step down at the same time as former General Manager Ian Campbell'. Actually there had been 'real problems', as Miller apparently did not appreciate the difference between chairing the board and running the company. Hugh Cunningham, who did, was delegated by his fellow board members to ask for Miller's resignation. He was replaced by Graham Prior, QC, Crown Solicitor, who came to SOSA with a solid background of committee experience with the Adelaide Festival of Arts.

Campbell stirred up a willy-willy in deciding to adopt Offenbach's original order of Hoffmann's doomed loves – Olympia the wind-up doll, Antonia the consumptive singer who dies for her art, Giulietta the mercenary courtesan – instead of what had become the common practice of keeping the most pathetic to the last. Being cheated of his amours in turn by magic, by avarice and finally by death allows Hoffmann's despair to grow in a logical sequence, but the arguments that followed Campbell's choice focussed attention on the work itself and the serious matters dealt with in an opera that tends to be judged on its effects rather than its substance. The casting of Judith Henley as Giulietta and Gillian Sullivan as Antonia came in for some questioning, one critic suggesting that they would have been better the other way round, and conductor Denis Vaughan was accused of taking the sparkle out of the score with some lugubrious tempi, but no quibbles were heard about how well suited Thomas Edmonds and Narelle Davidson were to their respective roles of Hoffmann and Olympia.

Ian Campbell and Rachel Gettler after their marriage, *Advertiser*, page 1, 13 September 1982

The Tales of Hoffmann opened in the Opera Theatre on Saturday, 11 September. Having a free day, and naturally well aware of the news value, that afternoon its director Ian Campbell married Carmen and Fiordiligi, a.k.a. Rachel Gettler, in the Adelaide Registry Office in a very private (Hugh and Margaret Cunningham were the witnesses and the only guests) ceremony. Upstaging his own production was not his intention – no, certainly not – one is forced to fit these things in around one's (in this case, two's) professional life (lives), and anyway the secret was not out until Monday. There had been many occasions during the former General Manager's six years with State Opera when he might have made the front page of the *Advertiser*. It took a wedding to get him there – with photograph. The gleeful grin on the bridegroom's face tells both of his joy at the event and his delight that, in one of the most gossipy towns on earth, he and his bride had been able to keep their secret. Always playing games, this man.

Mr and Mrs Campbell left Adelaide on 13 September for a honeymoon in Honolulu en route to New York. In the preceding week the former General Manager of State Opera privately recorded frank – sometimes brutally so – conversations with Alan Hodgson, a member of the Board and an experienced interviewer. When asked what he thought were his 'most significant achievements' he replied 'I survived and so did the company'. He recalled that on his arrival he expressed the hope that when he left he would 'give them back a better company than they gave me'. Most opera patrons would agree that he did.

Over the six years of his rule interest in the company's affairs as measured by local and interstate press coverage had multiplied by a putative factor of five. Its reputation within South Australia had won 4,247 subscribers in the peak year 1978–9 and had steadied around that mark, The Friends had another 1,000 members and attendances had peaked in 1981–2 at 92 per cent of theatre capacity, never going below 73 per cent. His repertoire had become steadily more mainstream but not even the sternest of professional and non-professional critics could accuse him of any lapse of taste or judgement. He had built up a core company of local singers, supplemented only as crucially necessary by imports, and had insisted on bringing into existence the State Opera Orchestra, the only alternative orchestra Adelaide had ever known. He could deal even-handedly with politicians of whatever persuasion, with the Board, with sponsors (though he admitted that his Patrons' Program had not worked), as well as with performers and production teams. He was too prickly, too opinionated, to be generally well liked – not long before he left Adelaide he was referred to as a 'trumped up little shit from New South Wales' and responded indignantly that he was a 'big shit' – but he didn't care, and he was certainly widely respected. He left behind a deficit of $126,000 in 1982, not regarded as unmanageable on a total turnover of $768,000.

His hopes for a top job at the Metropolitan Opera did not materialise, but in 1984 he found a niche at the San Diego Opera and has remained there as General Director ever since.

The impetus of Campbell's management survived his departure, and *Falstaff* attracted a handful of promotion features, including three – one local, one interstate and one national – on the director Colin George. Attendances were slightly down on the two previous seasons, going from over 90 per cent to around 86 per cent. Over the previous three years or so, a trend had been emerging among the critics showing that their judgements were becoming increasingly based on expectations of extremely high standards in all aspects of the production and performances. As the company made steady progress up the scale of professionalism, so the reviewers appeared to be keeping one step ahead. As it should be.

Taken overall, *Falstaff* was a more than respectable effort for a small company, and the points of adverse criticism dealt with refinements rather than generalities – James Christiansen could have been more roguish, Colin George seemed unfamiliar with the *opera buffa* tradition. For Kenneth Hince (*Age*, 1 November) '*Falstaff* had proved too complex and elusive for the company ... I could not find an effervescence of ensemble to match the pace and texture of the music'. And despite Denis Vaughan's claims to have discovered 27,000(!) discrepancies between Verdi's autograph and the printed score, his tempi and definition were taken to task by at least two well-informed writers. Musicological justification is no substitute for sound musical judgement.

Since the opening of The Opera Theatre in 1979 State Opera had been agitating, with government support, to get all its offices and the wardrobe workshop together on the same premises. In November, following purchases of other buildings nearby, the new facilities in Market Street in the centre of the city, plus a five storey carpark, were officially opened, and Jim Coogan's fantastical car, built for Dr Dulcamara and his *Elixir of Love*, was the first vehicle up the ramp into backstage at the theatre from the new loading area immediately behind. State Opera had outgrown the limited and frankly scruffy deconsecrated church at Hindmarsh that had been their working base since New Opera days. A smart outfit needed a smart home.

State Opera's Christmas present to its Youth Company and to Adelaide was a single performance of *The Childhood of Christ* by Berlioz. Dean Patterson conducted ninety singers and forty players, most of them still at school.

Larry Ruffell's first task was to announce the 1983 season – not his, because the relevant decisions would have already been made for him. Four operas only, down from five the previous year; no interstate tours; one Youth Company event (Kurt Weill's *Down in the Valley*), one less than in 1982. The choice of *Madame* (sic) *Butterfly*, *The Pearl Fishers* and *The Magic Flute* indicated that the company was aiming to play it even safer than before, but *The Rake's Progress* would console those who sought more exotic fare. In February Ruffell came into close contact with his fellow opera managers and their chairmen at a combined meeting in Melbourne to discuss matters of mutual concern – meaning, in plain terms, money, and how to make it go as far as possible. Apart from agreeing to assist each other to the maximum in sharing sets and costumes, the idea of a joint production for all states in 1985 was mooted. They also agreed to lobby for the resumption of federal funding to the regional companies, and this did eventuate – but not until 2000. Ruffell had some house-keeping to attend to at home. In late March he presided over bringing all the staff under the one roof in Market Street.

He must have felt that his first opera was a breeze. With the immensely popular Marilyn Richardson and the highly rated import John Main in the leading roles and a strong supporting cast, Puccini's tragic story of love and betrayal could not fail as a crowd pleaser. Nor did it – after the first two perfor-mances the remainder of the season was completely sold out. Some found the designs plain, even dull. Hugh Colman's bare, knotty pine platforms looked a bit as though the set was not quite finished, and Butterfly and Suzuki had to sing their lovely Flower Duet empty-handed because he gave them no flowers to scatter, but his gorgeous kimonos were as colourful as Puccini's orchestration. The principals, all experienced in stage craft, found their way around quite easily, but the chorus appeared in need of more specific direction. The Arts Council of SA toured the full production to Mount Gambier and Port Pirie in late May.

Interstate collaboration brought Victoria State Opera's sets and costumes for *The Pearl Fishers* to Adelaide in July. Interest in the first Adelaide perfor-mance of an opera whose sole claim to fame was a duet between two men persuaded State Opera to extend the season for an extra night, and with Marilyn Richardson as the beautiful, mysterious priestess, James Christiansen (her real life husband) as the priest who must condemn her to death, Roger Howell as the spurned lover and newcomer Gary Bennett as the winning one, popular success was guaranteed. David Gyger had followed the production as it travelled from Melbourne to Sydney to Perth to Adelaide, and having seen it and other versions six times was well qualified to pronounce judgement. He commended (*Opera Australia*, August 1983) all the principals and the chorus – 'some of the best ensemble singing I have yet heard from SOSA' – and conductor Denis Vaughan who 'turned in a thoroughly idiomatic and sensitive reading' of the score. James Renfrey (*News*, 4 July) gave State Opera yet another roasting for spending 'time, money and the splendid talents of its cast' on a piece which he believed had been justly neglected, for one thing because 'much of the music is commonplace and empty'.

Not words that anyone could possibly use about SOSA's next listing. *The Rake's Progress*, Stravinsky's translations of Hogarth's account in paintings of the terrible descent into madness and depravity of one Tom Rakewell. Robert Gard returned to portray the hapless Tom with the same veracity that had distinguished his Aschenbach, Gillian Sullivan was his always true love Anne Truelove, Lesley Stender appeared by courtesy of The Australian Opera as the bearded lady, Baba the Turk, and the young David Hibbard put another foot on the lower rungs of his ladder to an outstanding career as the Madhouse Keeper. Director Anthony Besch brought with him long experience of the piece, having worked at Glyndebourne alongside conductor Carl Ebert during his preparation of its première in Venice in 1951. It showed in every aspect of the sets – Anne's garden, Mother Goose's brothel, the churchyard and the final lunatic asylum – and in his deft placings of people and things within them. The poor, demented, barely human wrecks shuffling and slobbering about their prison were horrifyingly realistic. Not surprisingly, given the harsh plot and equally threatening music, the average attendance dropped to its lowest in State Opera's ten years, 64 per cent, but *The Rake* forged another link in the company's admirable chain of twentieth-century operas. Newly appointed Assistant Conductor Alexander Ingram displayed a firm, crystal clear, rock solid beat when he stepped in to make his debut in one of the performances.

The sophistication of the score and its production was enhanced by a splendid foyer exhibition of the Hogarth engravings, on loan from the City of Hamilton Art Gallery, alongside David Hockney's contemporary drawings on the same subject from the Art Gallery of Western Australia.

The Magic Flute is undoubtedly the silliest and most confused of Mozart's operas, but also the most popular. One day some really discerning, very brave director with a quirky sense of humour will present it as a pantomime complete with Principal Boy and Widow Twankey, and its philosophical maunderings will be revealed as circus acts. That time did not arrive with Colin George's orientalised costumes and his manner of playing up the *buffa* and playing down – *way* down – the *seria*. Attendances recovered to 85 per cent, but the reviews were mixed. Demanding as it does a number of quite rare voices, *The Flute* is not an opera to be cast in-house, especially for such a small company as State Opera. Some of the imports were well regarded – American bass Greg Ryerson's imposing Sorastro, Helen Adams bewitching as Pamina, Christopher Dawes a mean and nasty Monostatos – but Joanne Neal missed the pinging top F in the 'Queen of the Night' aria. Locals Thomas Edmonds (Tamino) and his bird catcher buddy Roger Howell met their targets, and the name of Grant Doyle first appeared as one of the Three Boys attending the dramatically challenged Queen. His career has continued to blossom as his sweet treble survived puberty to become an even sweeter baritone.

The productions proceeded, apparently smoothly, but behind the scenes concern was growing that the new General Manager was finding that taking charge of a largish opera company with big ideas in a city that saw itself, even in 1983, as Australia's state of opera, was vastly different from running a smallish dance company in the modest horizons of Canberra. By November, after what members have described as an extremely frank confrontation between the SOSA board and Larry Ruffell, matters had been resolved, and a press release with all the appropriate expressions of regret that he must return to Canberra (Ruffell) and of gratitude for his services (SOSA Board) announced that his appointment would terminate as from 1 December. Following Ian Campbell was never going to be an easy job, but some questions were asked as to whether his successor had been given a fair go. Thirteen months seemed a bit short.

10

Almost Consumed by
The Fiery Angel – 1984–87

❦

Musical chairs is a simple game, and the changeover from Myer Fredman to Denis Vaughan as Musical Director had taken place with comparative ease. But in the three years to December 1980 to 1983 State Opera was playing general post. Eight changes to senior positions – musical director, chairman of the board, general manager – occurred in this period. The machine kept whirring, the productions bumped in and bumped out, and no one without inside knowledge would have had any inkling that backstage and in the board-room dramas were being played out to rival the tension of those on stage. Much of the credit for keeping the main show on the road and keeping the support act out of the limelight was due to Andrew Pain. Nominally the company's Planning Manager but in reality carrying responsibilities beyond his brief, he officially took on the position of Acting General Manager from December 1983.

Larry Ruffell's precipitate departure from the top management position set the Board on the hunt once again. Following the company's successes, this position had become highly desirable, and a number of promising candidates were interviewed. The selection committee was not unanimous, but a majority eventually – after differences that became public knowledge – settled the matter. Ian Johnston, a project officer for the Music Board of the Australia Council, brought a background of administrative experience very similar to that of his predecessor but one, Ian Campbell. They shared a wide knowledge of opera itself and of the interesting ways of opera companies, but differed dramatically in their personalities. Johnston was reserved, sensitive, softly spoken and totally uninterested in drawing attention to himself, confident of his own judgement in artistic matters, happy to leave things that called for a measure of self-assertion, like sponsorship, to the Board.

The 1984 Adelaide Festival of Arts opera came to Adelaide with hefty baggage. *Lady Macbeth of Mtsensk*, first performed to great acclaim in Moscow in 1934, subsequently earned for its composer Dmitri Shostakovitch the wrath of Stalin himself, who was outraged by its overt sexuality (including a full scale seduction with music to match) and attacked the music as bourgeois and decadent. Shostakovitch took it underground, where it stayed until 1964.

Sensational stuff, and the press gave it a good run in the lead-up, offering teasers that the seduction scene would be played naked – or perhaps in body-stockings – either way the rehearsals were definitely closed – and making several mentions of 'pornophony', the term coined by Anon for Shostakovitch's music to copulate by. Director John Tasker, flamboyant by nature, was fully in tune with the work's power-driven exuberance, and Peter Cooke's designs and costumes stamped 'Russian' all over the stage. Conducting his first opera in Adelaide since 1974, Patrick Thomas told the terrible story of a beautiful woman's frustration, her brief fulfilment in illicit lust and final betrayal through the orchestra rather more effectively than Beverley Bergen (Katerina) and Ron Stevens (Sergei) did on stage. Sexual intercourse, except for the serious voyeur, is ludicrous to watch, and in spite of carefully choreographed heaving, rearing, thrusting and thrashing the passion stayed in the pit. Word got around that when he had done his duty in the last performance, Stevens got up off the bed and muttered 'Thank God that's over'.

In spite of the lurid baits *Lady Macbeth* pulled in only 68 per cent of Festival Theatre capacity; serious opera patrons are not likely to be won by sensationalism, and at that time Shostakovitch was still regarded with great suspicion as a difficult and alienating, if not downright ugly, composer.

As Ian Johnston moved into his new position at the end of March – Tony Kracmera described him (*Advertiser*, 7 April) as having 'the air of a bank manager ... but tough as nails' – Andrew Pain was appointed as his deputy. A wise move – major roles need a good cover.

Festival operas always consume a huge amount of the company's energy, and the following subscription seasons required extra nurturing to avoid a feeling of letdown, both on stage and in the auditorium. After the Russian extravaganza, *The Abduction from the Seraglio*, arguably Mozart at his most elusive, Beethoven's paean of praise to wifely devotion *Fidelio*, Handel's *Julius Caesar* and the dark tragedy of individuals caught up in a terrible war so eloquently portrayed by Verdi in *Il trovatore* added up to a pretty solid, pretty serious year.

And so it turned out. The light touch of Dennis Olsen's direction of the Mozart was generally admired, as were the sets, costumes and lighting of Alistair Livingstone. Although the comedy was played up to the maximum – some said 'and beyond' – unevenness in the casting resulted in the unlikely plot seeming even less credible, and some quite stringent criticism was levelled at conductor Denis Vaughan by Sam Hordern (*Australian*, 14 May) on the grounds that 'he seemed very insensitive to the soloists in this performance' and was not always able to ensure synchronisation between stage and pit. Larger audiences – they averaged only 60 per cent – would have helped to raise the level of excitement.

Colin George made his fifth foray to State Opera to direct Marilyn Richardson (Leonora), Alberto Remedios (Florestan), James Christiansen (Don Fernando), David Brennan (Don Pizarro), William Fleck (Rocco), Christine Douglas (Marcellina) and Geoffrey Harris (Jacquino) in a competently staged and sung *Fidelio*. Ralph Middenway, always a loyal and sympathetic supporter, was not pleased on the opening night and returned later in the season to make sure his complaints were valid. On his first visit (*Advertiser*, 23 June) he was offended because 'Colin George allowed or instructed Alberto Remedios to clank about the overlit stage in a hammy way ... revealing not a starving scarecrow but a pleasantly well-fed international opera star apparently filling in time waiting for the singing to start'. After his second visit he recapped (*Advertiser*, 28 June) his criticism, saying that 'It was unreasonable of State Opera to subject audiences to great patches of sloppy ensemble', and somewhat grudgingly conceded that the ensemble had improved, but not enough for his liking. Attendances were higher – averaging 80 per cent – than for the Mozart, probably because *Fidelio* is better known than *Seraglio* and Beethoven's brand name is well-nigh irresistible.

Press releases from Publicity Manager Christobel Chappell for the company's third venture into the highly specialised world of baroque opera, Handel's *Julius Caesar*, promised a 'grand spectacular' with 'lavish theatrical effects' such as 'clouds parting before a great mountain which opens up to reveal Cleopatra herself, seated in a temple and surrounded by the nine muses'. Tom Lingwood immersed himself in eighteenth-century operatic conventions to reproduce them as closely as possible in his sets and direction, and Peter Riley created magical transformations with his lighting. Lauris Elms sang Caesar with the range, if not exactly the quality, of a castrato, and although the production seemed unable to decide whether it was realistic or stylised, until The Australian Opera staged its famed account of the same piece in June 1994 SOSA's version, a joint exercise between State Opera and Victoria State Opera, created a new baroque benchmark for the country. Its musical standards, and those of *The Magic Flute* from the previous year, were recognised by their inclusion in the ABC's 1985 Showcase Series of broadcast operas.

Lauris Elms stayed on in Adelaide to play Azucena, the vengeful ancient gypsy at the core of *Il trovatore*, a role for which she had already been highly acclaimed. The sets and costumes were on loan from Lyric Opera of Queensland and James Christiansen directed. Verdi was served well by the big voices of Lauris Elms, Kenneth Collins (Manrico) and Margaret Haggart (Leonora) and by the chorus, grouped in solid phalanx for maximum impact. In his final engagement for the company before returning to Europe Denis Vaughan stuck to his musicological guns, insisting on implementing his discoveries of 'asymmetrical use of phrase signs and a discriminatory balance of certain instruments'. Neither critics nor performers were convinced. A happy coincidence brought the end of the *Trovatore* season together with the opening of the 1984 Italian Festival in South Australia, providing a perfect opportunity to declare the last performance a Gala night and follow it with a celebratory supper, which was well supported by Adelaide's large and operatically appreciative Italian community.

After serving for eleven years as New Opera's foundation chairman and subsequently on the boards of both New Opera and State Opera, Richard Brown retired. His contributions to the companies' affairs, especially in persuading prominent business men and women that opera was also a business and worthy of their practical and financial support, were warmly praised, and his love of the art form and his loyalty to the company had been (and remain) unflagging. Also making his final bow for State Opera in 1984 was Dean Patterson. As singer, director, member of various boards and committees and most recently as conductor, he was a central figure on and offstage, performing 15 different roles, starting with the Fox in *Chanticleer* for Intimate Opera in 1968 and finishing with *The Rime of the Ancient Mariner* for the State Opera Youth Company in 1984. Only when he moved interstate did his long and productive association cease.

As opera became more and more popular throughout the country, many people became aware that the national company (TAO) was getting what looked like huge federal subsidies that indulged the burgeoning appetites of Sydneysiders and occasionally Melbournites (all regarded as rich, snobbish and 'elitist', whatever that means) and left the rest of us in the BAPH (Brisbane, Adelaide, Perth and Hobart) states with no return for the taxes we had paid to support a national company that we never saw. It was a shallow and ill-informed argument. The federal subsidy was calculated to support a full-time company that would perform mainly in Sydney and spend three months each year in Melbourne, the two cities where the population was large enough to produce reasonable box office returns. But the complaints were taken seriously by the board and management of The Australian Opera, and investigations were initiated to consider ways in which co-operations with local authorities could allow more BAPH dwellers to see where their taxes were going. In Adelaide, the solution was for the Adelaide Festival Centre Trust to act as entrepreneur and underwrite the touring costs of TAO. Thus 1985 was billed as a joint season between the local and national companies with a total of eight operas, five of 'ours' and three of 'theirs'.

From the day the program was announced, one opera took centre stage, standing out well in front of State Opera's *Rigoletto, Don Giovanni, Manon* and *Countess Maritza*, and even upstaging the visiting *Aida, Tosca* and *Fiddler on the Roof*. The Australian première of Richard Strauss's *Capriccio* would have graced an Adelaide Festival, and here it was in a normal subscription season. What a sophisticated centre of opera we had become. Of course we were not to know then that our *Capriccio* would be the only one Australia would see live until the year 2000, when Sydney caught up with us once again.

Capriccio was Ian Johnston's first chance to prove his managerial worth, and his gumption and his good judgement were everywhere in evidence.

Anne Fraser's delectable sets and sumptuous gowns, lit with a golden glow by Jamie Lewis, were matched in both opulence and delicacy by the elegant hands (he never used a baton) of Georg Tintner, whose intimate knowledge and respect for the score worked magic with the singers – Beverley Bergen as the Countess, David Brennan as her brother, TAO Principal Artist John Pringle the poet and Geoffrey Harris the composer between whom she could not choose, James Christiansen the entrepreneur La Roche, Elizabeth Campbell the actress Clairon (which she sang again in Sydney fifteen years later) and William Bamford as Taupe, the prompter. The only factor beyond Johnston's control

John Pringle and Beverley Bergen, *Capriccio*, 1985

was the Adelaide Symphony Orchestra, excused in part for its lack of style by inadequate rehearsal, but held accountable for untidy ensemble.

Apart from the production, Johnston put the stamp of his personality on the printed program. It was a pleasure to read interesting short articles by writers who were not promoting themselves or the production but clearly knew what they were talking about – director Bernd Benthaak on the work's genesis, Tintner on the music, musicologist Andrew McCredie on the riddle of whether the music or the words were more important, and an unsigned appetiser, 'The Theme in Quotations' – was this our General Manager speaking? Yes it was, and in a most distinctive voice.

The pre-production press was lively – a major feature about John Pringle, who had sung his Olivier in Brussels and was off to Paris for repeats, a recipe for the fifteen-centimetre creamcake Daphne Harris had to gobble as the Italian opera singer and the promise of miniature ones in the intervals – but fear of the unknown kept all but the brave away, and the dismal figure of 59 per cent average attendances, the company's lowest ever, was recorded. Measured in purely artistic terms, though, *Capriccio* is still rated by many as State Opera's finest hour.

The rest of 1985 was comparatively risk-free. Michael Beauchamp's Fascist *Rigoletto* gave Roger Howell his first take on the wretched jester and Myer Fredman came back for Tom Lingwood's *Don Giovanni*, with Howell as Leporello and David Brennan in the title role. Christine Douglas continued her pursuit of stardom in what was billed as 'Nigel Triffitt's Massenet's *Manon*'; the settings and costumes, devised with as much intention of shocking the audience as elucidating the work were either 'striking' in their 'originality' (Michael Harrison, *Australian*, 14 October) or an infuriating mix of brilliance and sheer silliness. Alexander Ingram, conducting his last opera before returning to England, refused to be diverted from his true purpose, however outrageous the goings-on above his head.

If Ian Johnston's invitation to Triffitt for *Manon* was whimsical, or even as some said perverse, the team he assembled for the year's finale was inspired. David Kram, Dennis Olsen and Anne Fraser conducted, directed and designed separately and together a perfectly timed, wickedly funny *Countess Maritza* that enticed Yvonne, daughter of composer Emmerich Kalman, to come from

Helen Adams and Geoffrey Harris, *Countess Maritza*, 1985

Vienna to see for herself. Sparkling, lilting singing and playing and dancing from Rhonda Bruce (Maritza), Ron Stevens (Count Tassilo), Helen Adams (Lisa) and her car-miming partner Geoffrey Harris (Baron Zsupan), all deliciously dressed à la 1920s, outrageous over-acting by local *very* theatrical identities Russell Starke and Margery Irving, sets of surpassing stylishness and the State Opera Orchestra giving a passable impersonation of a gypsy band – very different from *Capriccio*, but in its own way just as satisfying.

Throughout the year Alexander Ingram had proved a lively and knowledgeable musical director and a conductor able to command respect and affection from his players and singers, and his conducting of the première of *The Snow Queen* by Adelaide composer Grahame Dudley with orchestrations by David Morgan gave the Youth Company its fourth successful event. Johnston's one major disappointment was that he had not been able to raise $50,000 to put on an Opera in the Park concert of *La Bohème*. Otherwise, he was entitled to be extremely proud of the first year that could be seriously regarded as his own work. From April he had been supported by his new chairman, former premier David Tonkin, whose enthusiasm for opera was comparable to his own.

For the 1986 Festival's major opera, TAO brought to Adelaide the première of Richard Meale's commissioned opera *Voss*. But as South Australia was celebrating its sesquicentenary, State Opera had its own commission. Twins Martin (composer) and Peter (librettist) from the Adelaide Wesley-Smith family created *Boojum*, a musical play based on the writings of Lewis Carroll. The opening on 10 March attracted a swathe of press about 'the Queen and the Stripper'; Her Majesty Queen Elizabeth II did attend, and she did see Sydney actor Waldemar Gorecki strip to his silver G-string for his song *I'm a Caterpillar of Society* and she did (according to him) enjoy it very much. So did the

The cast of *Boojum*, 1986. From left: Matthew Barker, Valerie Bader, Waldemar Gorecki, Trevor Sheean, Reg Ellery, Christine Douglas, Roger Howell, Jenny Vuletic, Moira Ross and Steven McLardie

audience, who took at face value a vaudeville grab-bag stuffed with everything from Alice in Wonderland to Carmen Miranda, accompanied by equally arbitrary music. But not *Boojum*'s parents. Within days of the opening, the composer had publicly (*Advertiser*, 15 March) accused the director of tampering with their offspring and making radical changes without consulting them. 'Treasured scenes had been cut completely, fundamental concepts had been changed, scenes had been moved ... *Boojum* was intended to be an audio-visual extravaganza', consistent with his reputation as an electronic composer. His intention was to 'demonstrate that area of my expertise by integrating it into a context of conventional toe-tapping music. I feel very miffed because it was a fundamental aspect of the creation and all that is left now is a few dinky little tunes ... My professional reputation is at stake based on decisions that had nothing to do with me.' Adelaide Festival of Arts artistic director Anthony Steel and the SOSA General Manager leapt to the defence of director Gale Edwards and her designers Mark Thompson and Ken Wilby, claiming that all she had done was to ensure the viability of the work. The critics defended the right of the Wesley-Smiths to be judged on their original vision. Kenneth Hince (*Age*, 13 March) thought the piece 'emerged ... with the air of a committee work ... with a feeling of impermanence, even of improvisation'; Michael Harrison (*Australian*, 12 March) described it as 'a series of sketches ... at one minute like a high school revue, at another Stephen Sondheim has his say', Ralph Middenway stated bluntly (*Advertiser*, 12 March) that '*Boojum* as an entity is not ready for paying audiences' and Brian Hoad (*Bulletin*, 25 March) saw it as 'absurdist theatre dealing with existentialist nihilism – Beckett with bells on and lots of party hats'.*

Intense lobbying from James Murdoch – he was seminal in the transformation of IOG into New Opera in 1972 – resulted in a 1986 Festival double bill of *The Glittering Gate* and *The Transposed Heads* of Peggy Glanville-Hicks. Three performances in the Playhouse were hailed more for the recognition they offered the composer, who attended them, than for their intrinsic merit.

---

*Seven years later Australian composer Vincent Plush reported (*Opera Australia*, April 1993) that *Boojum* had been performed as the Wesley-Smiths meant it to be in La Jolla, California, giving 'clear evidence of its stature as a masterpiece'.

Michael Shmith (*Age*, 22 March) wrote a splendidly perceptive interview with her, well-known for her refusal to be considered a 'woman composer'.

In June chairman David Tonkin resigned to take a position in London and was replaced by Alan Hodgson, a prominent broadcaster and board member since 1975. Keith Smith, well known for a number of prestigious business connections, was a new appointee. Staff changes brought Australian-born, European-trained (with the distinguished conductor John Pritchard, no less) Andrew Greene to replace Alexander Ingram as Music Director and Sioux Christiansen, daughter of James, as PR Officer. She set about popularising the company with a startling poster advertising

SEX INTRIGUE CORRUPTION
SEE IT LIVE AT THE OPERA

and letting people know that they could even wear jeans.

The first fully staged Wagner opera in Adelaide since *Tannhäuser* in 1968, *The Flying Dutchman* stood out as the most memorable production (*pace Boojum*) in 1986. In the pit with the Adelaide Symphony Orchestra John Matheson kept his promise to prove that Wagner's scoring actually favours voices as long as his directions are scrupulously followed. Beverley Bergen revelled in Senta as well she should have with Malcolm Donnelly as her darkly brooding Dutchman, and designers Ken Wilby and Mark Thompson created the most riveting illusion that both ships were anchored side by side in the bay. Many of Bernd Benthaak's touches – ghostly arms waving desperately through the port-holes begging for mercy, twitching bodies hanging from the yardarms – chilled the blood. A critic new to the scene ensured he would be noticed with a scornful reference to 'Senta's dreadful ballad' (Roger Knight, *Adelaide Review*, June 1986).

Memorable moments abounded in the latter half of the year – Fiona Maconaghie's Susanna in *The Marriage of Figaro*, variously described as 'pert', 'thrilling', 'effervescent' and 'miraculous'; Stuart Challender expertly conducting the Adelaide Symphony Orchestra while Christine Johnson rejected all traditional directorial notions of *Macbeth*; Lindy Hume's irreverent production of *The Italian Girl in Algiers* which left some deeply offended and others hooting with delight.

Apart from the mainstage operas, SOSA was active in schools and in concerts. In September, normally acerbic critic Peter Goers thoroughly enjoyed (*Advertiser*, 30 September) Christine Anketell's 'delightful and poignant production' of Malcolm Williamson's *The Happy Prince*, a joint enterprise between State Opera, Patch Theatre and Seacombe High School. In October Marilyn Richardson and James Christiansen gave a farewell recital prior to moving to Queensland. During the twelve years they had lived in Adelaide, between them they had contributed to 19 different productions. And State Opera played matchmaker for the second time in September when Macbeth (Roger Howell) married one of his witches, Felicity Baldock.

While SOSA's productions were proceeding apace, none less than respectable, some unarguably excellent, none of them dull, not a lot was being said publicly about the company's financial situation. In April 1986 Ian Johnston had announced that a planned season of *The Iron Man*, an opera for young people by local composer Malcolm Fox based on a story by Ted Hughes, had to be postponed because of a mounting deficit for the year, blamed at least in part on poor attendances for *Boojum*. The Fox-Hughes piece was performed by the State Opera Youth Company in April 1987 during the biennial Come Out Festival, giving a hundred or so young singers and players the chance to work with professionals of the highest calibre – conductor Brian Stacey, director Lindy Hume and designer Graham Maclean.

State Opera's *Madama Butterfly* looked even less artistic in the Festival Theatre than it had in the Opera Theatre in 1983, and Christa Leahmann's exaggerated efforts to make herself look Japanese severely cramped her singing and acting style, but the occasion was noteworthy on other counts. For the first time for this company, and for Adelaide, the brilliantly simple device of surtitles, a system that projects simultaneous English translations of the original text, in this case Italian, also a first, onto the proscenium arch above the stage, was employed. The advantages are many. The audience can follow all the nuances of meaning while the opera is being sung in its original language, the singers enjoy the immediate responses, especially to moments of humour, and as many Australian singers at this time were making reputations abroad in opera houses where the original language is the norm, State Opera could begin to engage principals, both native and foreign, without having to request that they re-learn their roles in English. The use of surtitles was a further step in the increasing sophistication and worldliness of the company.

Ian Johnston made no bones about his choice of *La Finta Gardiniera* (translated as *Sandrina's Secret*) – it was cheap. From the pen of Mozart at the age of eighteen, it neither looked or sounded cheap. Ken Wilby made an interesting debut as director, Andrew Greene conducted a score whose words and music he had spent much time in revising, and Deborah Riedel, born in the Barossa Valley, played her first major role – Arminda, described by her and others as a sort of Joan Collins of the eighteenth century – in Adelaide. Ian Johnston's fourth year in the top job ended as his first had begun, with a bold move into territory foreign to State Opera in 1987 but consistent with the policies of New Opera in 1973. Stephen Sondheim's *Sweeney Todd*, directed by Gale Edwards (another case of State Opera recognising outstanding talent in the

Set, Sweeney Todd, 1987

Lyndon Terracini, *Sweeney Todd*, 1987

bud) with frighteningly realistic sets by Wilby and Thompson and a mighty cast led by music theatre phenomenon Lyndon Terracini, legitimate theatre veteran Nancy Hayes and Greg Yurisich (another on the rise to an outstanding career) is still referred to as one of SOSA's most artistically successful events, standing alongside – or perhaps across the road from – the 1985 *Capriccio* for overall excellence.

Yet more staff changes occurred before year's end. David Kram, widely experienced in all genres of music theatre and generally a man of culture was appointed as State Opera's fifth musical director from 1 January 1988. He followed Myer Fredman, who went to Sydney after five years because he had had enough of coping with Adelaide, Denis Vaughan, who returned to Europe because Adelaide had had enough of coping with him, Alexander Ingram, who returned to England and for some time wished he had stayed in SA and Andrew Greene, who left to take up a Bayreuth scholarship and subsequent freelancing. Journalist Andrew Bolt joined the company as publicity officer in July, around the time that the Prostitutes Association of SA requested permission to send three of their members to each performance of *La traviata* to lobby for decriminalisation of their trade. It was a serious request, taken seriously, but rejected as being inappropriate for the company and the occasion.

1988 should have seen a continuation of Johnston's knack for picking repertoire that advanced Adelaide's operatic taste instead of merely re-inforcing it and his nose for young singers and directors with big potential.

Fate ordained otherwise.

11

$\mathcal{B}$ronco $\mathcal{B}$ill

to the $\mathcal{R}$escue – 1988–94

$\diamond$

$\mathcal{G}$eorge's festival', the 1988 Adelaide Festival of Arts was and still is known as.

Central to Lord Harewood's choices, all of them made with encyclopedic knowledge and impeccable (except when you disagreed with him) judgement, was Prokofiev's rarely performed study of derangement and disillusionment, most aptly named *The Fiery Angel*.

The artistic director named the work as one of his most favoured in all the repertoire, and getting it staged in Adelaide gave him enormous personal satisfaction. It did the same for State Opera, who claimed this treasure as their own, and were justly proud to collaborate with a number of eminent visitors. From England came director David Pountney to work with local (almost SOSA resident) designers Mark Thompson and Ken Wilby, Josephine Barstow, billed as one of the few sopranos in the world capable of making musical and dramatic sense out of the demented, obsessive heroine Renata, and Stuart Kale for four cameos demanding a more than usually robust tenor. New Zealander Rodney Macann played the disturbed hero Ruprecht and Australians Irene Waugh, Gregory Yurisich and Beverley Shean filled in the story with eight small but crucial characters. Stuart Challender conducted, and David Kram carried the weighty load of getting the cast and the Adelaide Symphony Orchestra ready for him.

Provocative on all fronts – music, plot, designs, direction – *The Fiery Angel* left the audiences and critics gasping for words to describe the work and its realisation, and fierce arguments raged throughout the season. A near disaster in rehearsal, when the stunt man standing in for Macann – literally on fire with unrequited love – found his exit blocked, put the emergency procedures to the test, relieved many minds and promised an extra thrill to the patrons.

Emergency procedures of a rather different kind were being prepared while the fiery angel of madness and despair was consuming Renata and Ruprecht and a small boy called Jake. The season closed on 14 March. On the previous day the *Sunday Mail* published an unsigned article headed 'State Opera in Close Threat'. The text stated that the company might have to shut down for a year and that its board and management were under threat of dismissal over a deficit of $500,000 which had only come to light in the previous two weeks. The matter attracted unprecedented press coverage. Research has turned up more than thirty pertinent articles published over the following few months, including one quoting the Opposition Agriculture spokesman accusing the premier of being prepared to bail out the opera company when 'nothing is being done to extend water west of Ceduna' (*News*, 11 April). The Premier made a ministerial statement (*Hansard*, 23 March) explaining that the company's deficit had occurred through 'an overambitious program, poor box office results and an inability to adjust workforce members in line with the 1987/88 budget allocation'. Mr Bannon also reported that he had 'asked the General Manager to consider his future'.

As far as the public knew, Ian Johnston was the villain of the piece. After protracted negotiations over his unfinished contract and his agreement that he would not discuss the matter for thirty years – thirty? that's how long Queen Elizabeth the Queen Mother was required to keep mum about the Duchess of Windsor! – he left. The SOSA board offered to resign but the government decided against further bloodletting and settled for a change of chairman, from Alan Hodgson to Keith Smith, already a board member. A strong suspicion emerged that Johnston was being scapegoated; the total deficit had actually been accumulating since 1982, when the annual report recorded a loss of

Josephine Barstow and Ken Moroney, *The Fiery Angel*, 1988

$126,000. Then a further $260,00 was lost the next year, and another $364,000 the next; in whatever way the accounts were presented, it was clear that successive boards had not taken seriously their responsibilities to ensure good financial management, and were therefore also culpable. If the board knew, then naturally the Department of the Arts also knew, and could have been expected to take some action. In the Annual Report of Year ended 30 June 1988 (a sober document on plain white paper, no glossy pictures, no rapturous, carefully selected quotes from the previous year's productions) the new chairman stated

> During 1987 the Board had become increasingly concerned about the quality and accuracy of financial information being provided. The Board in fact requested that the year-end accounts 1986/87 be re-presented ... since in their initial form it was not possible to determine a true picture of the financial state of the company.

In fact those accounts showed an accumulated deficit of $1,356,000 at 30 June plus a new deficit for the year of $202,000, in total $1,558,000.

Whatever the actual debt, and whoever was to blame, it was insupportable. The 1988 program was pretty well in place and would have cost more to cancel than to implement. But subsequent years would be lean, with fewer productions and therefore less demand for services at all levels of administration and production. Fearful for their jobs, the staff campaigned against the board, expressing their lack of confidence in the members – four arts people, three business – and calling for them to be replaced by people with better knowledge of administration and finance. They were right to be concerned. Some left almost immediately, others, some very long-serving like secretary Lorna Matthews, were told their positions no longer existed. Phillip Virgo, on a year's contract as Marketing Manager, was sacked one morning. The same afternoon he was re-hired by Finance Consultant Nigel Bray (widely believed to have been the one who got to the bottom of the company's black hole of debt) to complete his plans for major fundraising events, one being the grand ball celebrating the *Carmen* season in October. It made $20,000. Just as well he stayed.

It was all pretty sad. A feeling developed that the government had over-reacted, that the decifit was no worse, relatively speaking, than The Australian

Opera had accumulated and traded out of in the '80s and '90s, when their problems had resulted in close scrutiny that concluded that the company had actually managed its finances extremely efficiently and that it was entitled to more, not less, subsidy. At the time of SOSA's troubles, and in hindsight, some sympathy swung behind Ian Johnston. Michael Harrison put into words (*Australian*, 12 May) what many were thinking. Referring to the measures insisted upon as a quid pro quo for the government's loan, variously quantified but most likely $800,000 to be repaid over three years, he wrote:

> Mr Johnston, the victim of the 'remedial action', will be a loss to the company in many ways. Under his leadership the State Opera provided a diverse and innovative choice of repertoire. As well as the customary Bohèmes and Butterflies, Adelaide opera lovers were treated to stylish and exciting productions of *Capriccio*, *Sandrina's Secret* and, of course, the splendid *Sweeney Todd*, which was staged last year.

Exactly. Incidentally one of the many unfair accusations levelled against Johnston was that he had failed to capitalise on that production by taking it on tour. Why? Because Melbourne Theatre Company did its own production, and opened on the night SOSA's closed. From all reports Melbourne did not come within a meat pie of Adelaide.

The show had to go on, nevertheless, and did with *The Letters of Amalie Dietrich*, a commissioned piece from local composer Ralph Middenway and librettist Andrew Taylor. Presented as a work in progress in the company studio in April, it gave to a small invited audience insights into the meaning of emancipation for a nineteenth-century woman botanist and also reminded all concerned of their responsibilities regarding the promotion of Australian music theatre.

In May Justin Macdonnell, Administrator of New Opera 1973 to 1976, was brought in to tide things over while a new chief executive was sought. No thank you, he did not want the job permanently. Definitely no. In fact he did not want it temporarily either, but was persuaded by Len Amadio and Alan Hodgson that he and he alone could sort things out. He identified incompetence at both management and staff level, was critical of the lack of supervision exercised and recommended drastic pruning of the company's operations, including closing the inefficient workshop and shedding a number of staff, among them some that he had appointed during his own tenure. His most important goal was to persuade the government that the company was salvageable and to draw up a plan for recovery. Central to that plan was the appointment, as soon as possible, of a new general manager.

Macdonnell and State Opera did not have to wait long. William (Bill) Gillespie, a 37-year-old American with extensive experience of opera in academic and practical settings, had come to Australia as a tourist in 1986, visiting Sydney and Melbourne and establishing contacts with like minds. In early 1988 he was working at Pittsburgh Opera when Ian D Campbell and Ken McKenzie Forbes from VSO both phoned with news of SOSA's plight. By April he had collected the background papers and had signified his interest in the General Manager position – even offering to pay his own fare to Adelaide for an interview. He met the board on a Monday in early June, went to see *Orpheus and Eurydice* on Tuesday, met his first koala at Cleland National Park on Wednesday, had lunch with Macdonnell on Thursday and that night went to the opera again to look backstage (the stage manager said 'Who are you?'), met the board again on Friday and did an interview with Tim Lloyd at the *Advertiser* just in case he got the job – actually he already had it – and flew back to Pittsburgh on Saturday. A week later his appointment was announced and on 25 July he started work. Nicknamed 'Bronco Bill' by the *Advertiser*'s gossip columnist Basil Arty, he welcomed an 'adventure to move 10,000 miles and rebuild an opera company from the ground up', in his words from an interview ten years later.

The 1988 program proceeded as planned. In a collaboration between SOSA and the ASO Nicholas Braithwaite conducted a semi-staged version of *Die Walküre* Act 1 with the orchestra in Hunding's backyard. Thomas Edmonds returned after two years of productive work and study in Europe for Gluck's *Orpheus and Eurydice* but had to cancel at late notice when stricken with laryngitis. Bernard Hull stepped in, and saved the show, but nothing could save the production. Thompson and Wilby went berserk in search of baroque authenticity – Roger Knight's review (*Adelaide Review*, July 1988) was headed 'I Have Lost my Orpheus' – leaving such indelible impressions as Rosemary Boyle as Amor with a Spanish galleon on her head. The same designers interpolated weird scenery and bizarre costumes and coiffures between *The Barber of Seville* and Rossini's audiences in the renamed Her Majesty's Theatre. Tristram Cary (*Opera Australia*, September 1988) dubbed them 'Wilby and Thompson, Stage Outfitters: Operas Decorated and Directed: Amazing Costumes a Speciality'.

In the *Barber* program Bill Gillespie issued in his first Message from the General Manager the timely reminder 'State Opera will be here tomorrow if you care today.'

Gillespie must have wondered if fate was feeling less benign in October when he had to find not one, not two, but three Carmens. State Opera's original choice, Margaret Russell, fell ill and was replaced by Jolanta Nagajek. She in turn succumbed, and Kirsti Harms left Mercedes to the cover and stepped up to Carmen. Russell three, Nagajek three, Harms two – not an easy run, and the new GM had to arbitrate in spats between the designers (W and T again, but this time kept in check by director Stuart Maunder) and the music director over the hiring of a troupe of flamenco dancers, but *Carmen* sold 90 per cent over its eight performances. His first year ended smoothly, and with a salutory reminder of his predecessor's penchant for operetta. For Lehár's *Paganini* Ian Johnston had assembled a custom-built production team of David Kram, Dennis Olsen – the world's only singing, acting, dancing, piano-playing opera director – and designer James Ridewood, and an utterly captivating cast led by Greg Tomlinson and Anne-Maree McDonald. Some critics continued their run of sneering at the froth and frivolity of the genre, dismissing operetta as beneath the dignity of both subsidised companies and themselves. Sourpusses, all of them.

Two operas only was the government's limitation imposed on Adelaide's beleaguered company for 1989, and as cheap as possible. *Fidelio* was borrowed from The Australian Opera (and gave Gillespie his chance to show that he had flair as well as everything else – the 1989 season was launched by the Premier in the Adelaide Gaol) and *La Bohème* from Victoria State Opera; both played in the Festival Theatre, Beethoven filling to 71 per cent capacity and Puccini (most notable for the return to Adelaide of Michael Lewis as Marcello after 17 years developing a fully professional career) to 80 per cent. The new GM succeeded in his campaign to bring in new audiences, some of them proving their innocence by chatting and taking flash light photographs during the performance. By second interval the *Bohème* cast were so fed up they threatened that if the flashing did not stop, the show would. The offenders desisted, but had no idea why they should.

So that opera patrons would not be too aggrieved at getting only two 'hits' (coined by Basil Arty) of their favourite art form, early in the year SOSA put on a season of opera films and a Gala Concert. The fact that Western Mining Corporation agreed to fund the latter as part of a generous three-year package can be taken as proof of Gillespie's powers of persuasion and as an indication that sponsors had not entirely lost faith in the company's ability to survive. WMC's lead in this regard was crucial both in restoring the company's self esteem and reassuring fellow companies that their investments would be well-founded.

With a little ($500,000) help from their friends in the state government, the Adelaide Festival Centre played host in the second half of the year to The Australian Opera's productions of *Cavalleria Rusticana* and *Pagliacci* and *The Gondoliers*. Evidence from other cities suggests that most opera patrons do not discriminate between different companies and just pick and choose the operas that appeal to them. Four operas, a concert, a master class, a costume sale and films – one wonders how many even realised how dramatically different 1989 was from 1988.

By the end of his first year, Gillespie was able to give back $100,000 to Treasury, cutting costs by paring staff to bare bones, closing the workshop and the wardrobe and exercising all his well-trained charm on sponsors. The State Opera Orchestra, never more than ad hoc, was no longer needed because the Adelaide Symphony Orchestra was playing for all productions – though not until 1996 were pit services formally written into its funding agreement with the government. The Education program took 52 performances of *Sid the Serpent who Wanted to Sing* by Malcolm Fox to 12,000 children in metropolitan and country schools and kept four singers, a one-man-band pianist and a stage-manager-cum-truck driver in work that led to a grand finale at Roxby Downs in the far, far north.

SOSA took great pride in its capacity to provide a training ground for local young singers and repetiteurs, gradually seeing them work up through the ranks of competence and responsibility. In early 1989 it became evident that many of them had been so well-trained that they were being poached by the other companies, some for the next rung of training as cadets, others for direct entry into the profession. Within the space of a year or so, twenty musicians – singers, pianists, conductors – and administrators had left Adelaide to take up positions in Sydney and Brisbane, both cities offering more performing opportunities and more specialised tertiary opera courses than were available in Adelaide. Public airing of the question in the press in February provoked a letter from James Christiansen (*Advertiser*, 9 March) claiming that the arts drain was caused by dwindling opportunities for employment and accusing 'those charged with creating and maintaining a healthy arts environment' of 'a grave dereliction of duty' in failing to heed warnings of State Opera's inevitable financial crisis. Blaming the government for undervaluing the arts was a rather fashionable pastime in 1989. Reminders of the extremely generous measures taken to ensure that State Opera survived usually won the argument.

Adelaide's unique record of distinguishing its Festivals with Australian premières of major twentieth century operas lapsed in 1990 because TAO had a new *Tristan und Isolde* and artistic director Clifford Hocking wanted it. After a bit of a spat between him and the national company's artistic director Moffatt Oxenbould over the use of surtitles – Hocking said Adelaide didn't need them (thank you, but he was too kind) – Oxenbould said my *Tristan* comes with surtitles or not at all – and that was that.

State Opera and the Festival co-produced the year's opening event, the city's first Opera in the Park, a single open air performance on 2 March of *Tosca* with Joan Carden doing her first Floria (her next in Adelaide was a decade later) and John Shaw his 354th Scarpia. 20,000 people were entranced with them and with Bruno Sebastian lamenting *E lucevan le stelle* to a balmy, star-studded autumn sky. Lyric Opera of Queensland lent their production of *Aida* for five performances in May, notable for the appearance of the very young, enormously promising Daniel Sumegi as the King of Egypt and Michael Lewis as Amonasro. With the assistance of surtitles audiences were becoming increasingly demanding of dramatic, as well as musical, conviction. Despite her reputation, Rita Hunter as Aida was inadequate on both counts. But she was a legend, and people came to see for themselves in such numbers that the 1989/90 annual report (shiny again) was able to include a proud photograph of John Bannon, Keith Smith and Bill Gillespie congratulating themselves on the large cheque wiping out the advance that had kept the company afloat. And there was more – the balance sheet showed a surplus of $391,000. It was a truly remarkable turnaround in only two-and-a-half years, which appeared to justify the extreme measures taken to achieve it. Whether the heart-ache caused by lost jobs was also justified is a question that will remain as long as there are people to ask it.

William Gillespie, John Bannon and Keith Smith, 1990

Much admired repetiteur David McSkimming moved up in his profession and over the border to Victoria State Opera in February and was replaced by accomplished Romanian musician Florin Radulescu, whose fluency in Italian, German and French was crucial for a company now consistently presenting operas in their original languages.

By June 1990 the Board had been strengthened in numbers and expertise. Alan Hodgson retired after thirteen years along with Robert Dahlenburg and Ian Brice; Christopher Hamilton and Mary Handley continued to represent the Friends and new appointees Timothy O'Loughlin, John Lovering, Paula Nagel, Maureen Mudge and Jonathon Richards brought a wealth of administrative experience, backed in most cases by a strong but also pragmatic view of the importance of opera and its place in modern society.

In July came what was nicknamed the baby *Figaro*. Eight mainly young singers, including Douglas McNicol, Deborah Peake-Jones and Roger Howell, all of whom have since developed into artists of significant stature, made role debuts in an intimate and intelligent production directed by Robyn Nevin, the highly respected actor and director from the world of straight theatre, and conducted by David Kram in Her Majesty's (a.k.a. Opera) Theatre. The naiveté and directness of the performers and Hugh Colman's realistic sets offended some and delighted others, and its readily understood story and irresistible music moved the secretary of Actors' Equity, Stephen Spence, to round up 500 unionists to attend a working dress rehearsal.

In spite of the debt being cleared, the policy of bringing in sets and costumes from other companies continued in October 1990 with *Samson et Dalila*, a co-production with VSO using gear from a co-production between San Francisco Opera and Lyric Opera of Chicago, and in March 1991 with Lyric Opera of Queensland's *Rigoletto* both in the Festival Theatre. David Porcelijn exercised exemplary discipline over the latter in the pit, Michael Lewis wrung the heart as the betrayed cripple and Patrick Power was the heartless yet seductive Duke. Some controversy was aroused by the introduction of much extraneous and unrelated business by director Garth Scott-Annetts, and after the relatively sympathetic acoustic of Her Majesty's Theatre, the singers and listeners were even more aware of just how dry and unresponsive the Festival Theatre was. Even Rita Hunter in *Aida* could not get its welkin to ring for her.

A nearly new, once-used, production of *Don Giovanni* by Jean-Pierre Mignon with designs by Kenneth and Victoria Rowell was lent by VSO after a Melbourne season paying tribute to the 200th anniversary of Mozart's death. The shock of Lyndon Terracini blazing onto the stage in very tight black tights, gold chains tangling with his primordial hairy chest, and black locks curling over his bare shoulders etched the impression deep into long-term memory – as did his perfectly timed impersonation of a randy but ever so refined goat.

In June 1991 Gillespie's contract was renewed for a further three years. Following the departure of David Kram after *Samson et Dalila* the Board made the momentous decision to abolish the post of Musical Director, begun with Myer Fredman in 1975, in favour of appointing a separate conductor for each production. The advantage of this system is that it enables specialised needs to be matched with specialists. The disadvantage is the loss of continuing supervision of the company's musical development, especially in regard to the nurturing of young voices. To compensate, Gillespie was designated General Director, a term coined initially in the USA to indicate both managerial and artistic authority. Gillespie's increased artistic responsibilities left the company with a gap which was plugged in early 1992 by creating a new position of Director of Productions. Stephen Phillips came to Australia from England in 1973 with theatre in his blood and a solid knowledge of music and opera, and got his first job at the Sydney Opera House in the same year. Having the inestimable advantage of being able to read music and find his way around complex opera scores, he soon moved into stage management with The Australian Opera, learning his trade on the spot and making friends and influencing people in the opera world as he went. Already well respected nationally in the profession when he came to Adelaide in 1989, Phillips was rapidly accepted into the local company and the community.

After two very lean years living on borrowings from its neighbours, in 1992 SOSA was ready to stand on its own productorial feet again. *Elektra*, composed in 1909 by Richard Strauss and one of his most admired, most difficult and most controversial operas, had never been performed in Australia. Here was a chance for another major coup with which to attract a great deal of attention from the media and from opera buffs around the country. And an ostentatious proclamation that the company had not only survived its vicissitudes but had emerged from them stronger than ever. The production team and the singers were all chosen to maximise both artistic and financial returns. Film director Bruce Beresford, reported to have a burning passion for opera, designer John Stoddart, conductor Richard Armstrong and singers Marilyn Zschau and Yvonne Minton were all names calculated to arouse great enthusiasm from the cognoscenti, and the gory story of violent revenge and assassination by axe within a violently disturbed family attracted both aficionados and novices, to the extent that the box office reported 94 per cent capacity in the Festival Theatre and the last two of the four performances were sold out. Once again Adelaide had pipped the eastern states. Not until 2000 did Sydney see *Elektra*, and then in a production from Berlin. The Adelaide people who made a special trip opined with some hauteur that they preferred their own.

Andrew Sinclair's production of *Madama Butterfly* in October brought to Adelaide conductor Richard Bonynge for his SOSA debut, John Pringle for his masterly Sharpless and Yoko Watanabe as the delicate geisha with a spine of steel. The season was sold out. Roger Knight (*Adelaide Review*, November 1991) was deeply moved – 'Frankly, I never thought I would ever see this preposterous old tear-jerker so affectingly done.'

Another superb team was assembled for the 1992 Adelaide Festival of Arts production of *Nixon in China* by John Adams. David Porcelijn, who had made

John Wegner, Australian Dance Theatre, *Nixon in China*, 1992

his first appearance in Adelaide as Musical Director of the Nederlands Dance Theatre in the 1986 Festival was now at the head of the ASO, Gale Edwards, building a formidable reputation as director of productions around the country and overseas and choreographer Leigh Warren, highly respected for his work with local modern dance companies put together a show that was deemed by those entitled to express an opinion to have actually improved on the original in Houston, Texas, whence came the sets and costumes, complete with the Spirit of 76 plane that landed ker-plop from the flies in the skies with Richard (James Maddalena) and Pat (Eileen Hannan) Nixon, Henry Kissinger (John Wegner being uncharacteristically vile) and their entourage for the re-enactment of their historic visit to China in 1972 and their meetings with Chairman Mao Tse Tung (Geoffrey Harris), his wife (Merlyn Quaife) and Chou En Lai (Mark McSweeney). A landmark for State Opera and also another first for opera in Australia, *Nixon* was seen only in Adelaide. Hailed as (at last) an opera that was about more than just lust and revenge and had some political relevance to our own times, it was also the last in Adelaide's long and illustrious run of exclusive showings of major twentieth-century operas. It was wonderful while it lasted, that run, and greatly missed when its race was over.

Any soprano who takes on Lucia di Lammermoor in Australia is bound to be measured against the yardstick of Joan Sutherland, who made the role her own and played it in Adelaide in a memorable matinée in 1980. (She said once she particularly loved singing matinées because the audience, many of them elderly, were there because they really wanted to be.) In the very same production in May 1992, and with the very same conductor, the eminently well-qualified Richard Bonynge, Patrick Power (Edgardo), Conal Coad (Raimondo) and John Bolton-Wood (Enrico) were so much more confident in their roles than Malvina Major that they, rather than the hapless heroine, stood out as the major figures. Her expressive range was severely limited – in the great Mad Scene she looked, according to one critic, merely cross.

Gale Edwards aroused the ire of many with her production of *The Magic Flute*. Roger Knight violently objected (*Adelaide Review*, September 1992) to her concept as 'the dream of a wealthy young socialite whose girlfriend has just walked out on him after finding a tart in his bed' and found her interpretation – 'little more than a narrow, chauvinistic paean to male dominance in marriage' – 'vulgar and mean-spirited'. Similar reactions had greeted the première in Melbourne for the VSO in 1991. Greg Tomlinson (Tamino) was generally commended, Judith Henley sang her first Pamina, a number of young local singers made role debuts in Mozart's serio-comic masterpiece and nearly 3,000 school children attended special 'look-in' presentations.

Surprise was expressed that Adelaide was seeing *Otello*, Verdi's unequalled study of manipulation through jealousy, for the first time, but voices that can cover the range and passion of the Moor, and actors who can make the evil Iago credible are rare. In the event, it was Malcolm Donnelly playing his first Iago who won most acclaim, and Peter Robinson's conducting was much admired.

Leaving aside *Nixon in China*, 1992 was artistically not the company's best year, but Gillespie was able to announce that subscriptions had increased by 10 per cent over the previous year.

The pattern of three mainstage operas per year, plus optional extras such as a *Madama Butterfly* in the park (March 1993, the first outside Festival time and rewarded by an attendance of 20,000), and a concert by Victoria de los Angeles in association with Andrew McKinnon and Associates the following June became the norm for the company.

Evidence of just how wide its horizons and how secure its base had become showed in three new productions – more than ever welcome after the re-cyclings of previous years – for the 1993 season. First up was a co-production of *Tosca* with Welsh National Opera; Marilyn Richardson a wonderfully petulant diva, Kenneth Collins from The Australian Opera in perfect Puccini voice for Cavaradossi, Sigmund Cowan rather too gentlemanly for an audience accustomed to the nasty, brutish hypocrisy of John Shaw. In his first opera (as for Bruce Beresford with *Elektra*) Sydney born, internationally noted theatre director Michael Blakemore worked on sets by Ashley Martin-Davis – somewhat perverse, observed several critics, to reduce the Madonna to a pair of feet in Act I, and to leave the key on the floor where anybody could have found it. John de Main, already known in Adelaide by reputation for his Houston première of *Nixon in China*, met the ASO and the company from the podium for the first time, delivering the passionate score in full measure. The techs and mechs, doubtless inspired by the speed and accuracy of the action on stage, managed to cut their scene changes down from 35 to 28 minutes and were duly rewarded (with booze, according to an unauthenticated report) by management.

The world also came to State Opera in August for Verdi's *Macbeth*. Tito Capobianco, General Director at Pittsburgh Opera, arrived with his designer Albert Filoni to direct, and Dutch conductor David Porcelijn presided over the pit. Michael Lewis (another debut) and Marilyn Zschau were cast as the vaultingly ambitious Scottish nobles and Conal Coad as Banquo. By chance, Rodney Milnes, editor of *Opera* magazine in London, was in Adelaide at the right time and reviewed *Macbeth* himself in place of the journal's regular SA critic. In an extensive report to his readers on opera all over Australia (*Opera*, November 1993) he took a dim view of us. 'The new *Macbeth* ... was the only performance of the trip that I disliked, and disliked intensely; wretchedly cut, ... drearily designed, limply directed ... and even more limply conducted by David Porcelijn, a distinguished conductor of twentieth-century music who sounded completely at sea in early Verdi.' Bill Gillespie had been miffed by previous critical notices from the local correspondent, but after the verdict delivered by

Mr Milnes, with whom even the most rash do not argue, decided she (Elizabeth Silsbury) was not so bad after all. The production was shipped off in early 1994 to Pittsburgh, Pennsylvania for its 1995–1996 season.

While the *Macbeth* season was still playing, State Opera and The State Theatre Company's Magpie Theatre collaborated in a novel event for children. Into a three-hour session were packed abridged versions of the play and the opera of *Macbeth*, both presented within Filoni's set on the Festival Theatre stage.

1993's final production was *Carmen*, also in conjunction with VSO. Director (Keith Warner) and conductor (Stephen Barlow) were both imported from England, and Dubravka Zubovic (Dalila from 1990) returned from her native Yugoslavia for the gypsy cigarette girl cum smuggler. Warner's determination to show her as a universal and timeless victim were not entirely successful, but his direction of the quintet at Carmen's soppy admission that she could not go a-smuggling with them that night because she was in love had them falling off their chairs with hysterics and whetted the appetitite for a full comedy from a director with such an eye for fun.

In June 1993 chairman Keith Smith reported that the company had completed its financial year with a surplus for the fifth year out of the preceding six, a modest $3,000, but highly commendable, given the strictures imposed on the company in 1988.

Christopher Hunt, Artistic Director of the 1994 Adelaide Festival of Arts, chose his program around the theme of bringing Australian and Asian cultures together, leaving no room for a major twentieth century opera. His preliminary announcement that his Festival would not have much room for local arts companies, and that there was not enough money for an opera, must have been a disappointment to State Opera, but also something of a relief. Festival operas had a nasty way of exceeding their budgets by large amounts, usually leaving the home team carrying the deficit. SOSA greeted Hunt's notice by stating that it was unlikely to be able to afford a festival opera in any case.

Timothy Sexton, chorus master for many of the preceding productions, took the full musical responsibiity for an expertly directed (Christine Anketell) and designed (Victoria Lamb) *Hansel and Gretel*, which played to more than 11,000 children in March and April in metropolitan schools and also made a special trip to Roxby Downs. Vanessa Benger and Jennifer Kneale were the two waifs, Timothy Sexton was Father, Wendy Hopkins Mother and Sandman and Brian Gilbertson the wicked and wickedly funny Witch.

Regular turnover of Board members had by this time become standard practice. By June 1994 mining and oil company executive Timothy O'Loughlin had replaced Keith Smith as chairman, the Friends, subscribers, sponsors and patrons elected Smith and their long-time treasurer and skilled costume maker Doris Brokensha to represent them, John Lovering's position went to Melanie de Crespigny and Lillian Scott, Paula Nagel and Sarah Smith stayed put. The list of Honorary Life Members was growing, comprising Richard Brown, Hugh Cunningham, Keith Smith and Kathleen Steele Scott. The permanent staff had been pared down to a mere seven, with Stephen Phillips having the position of Deputy General Director added to his production responsibilities.

Entrepreneur Andrew McKinnon is passionate about singers and their songs, and in spite of poor audiences he persisted in organising national tours for famous international soloists at their peak – or in some cases slightly past it. The recital of acclaimed soprano Teresa Berganza, a joint venture between McKinnon and State Opera, drew only 700 to the Adelaide Town Hall in April, but they were enthralled by her voice and her distinctive interpretations.

Perhaps the patrons were saving up for SOSA's loan from Lyric Opera of Queensland, *La traviata*, which was so popular that an extra performance had to be scheduled. Judith Henley literally dazzled the opening night audience with a $1 million diamond necklace courtesy of Adelaide jeweller and SOSA board member Albert Bensimon. It came with its own security guard, and was replaced after its scintillating première by the more customary costume jewellery – value? about $29. Henley and her Alfredo, Geoffrey Harris, shone rather less brilliantly than her necklace, and it was Neville Wilkie's Germont that drew most praise.

The sopranos who dominated *Adriana Lecouvreur* and *Salome*, both borrowed from The Australian Opera, were not South Australians. Patiently, the company continued to explain to politicians agitating on behalf of local singers who believed that their talents were being overlooked in favour of imports that special roles can only be filled by special voices, and in many cases at any one time there are only a handful of them all over the world capable of measuring up to the required musical and dramatic standards. Explanations were accompanied by evidence that no, the locals were not overlooked. They were looked over, and when they passed muster they were employed.

Rodney Macann, Marilyn Zschau,
Salome, 1994

Yoko Watanabe was just as strong in the doubly dramatic role of the actress Adriana as her fragile Butterfly had been in 1991. Andrew Sinclair's staging of the original by John Copley missed many opportunities for intensifying the drama of Adriana's real-life amours, but Richard Bonynge inspired the Adelaide Symphony Orchestra, realising Cilea's lush score so effectively that the ears always knew the state of play, even if the eyes were left in some uncertainty.

Distinguished conductor Edward Downes, an authority on the music of Richard Strauss, had been booked to conduct *Salome*, but was replaced at short notice by David Stanhope, fresh from the same job in Sydney. Adelaide had always been proud of this multi-gifted player and scholar, and his management of the ASO, augmented to 95, showed his understanding both of the complex score and his empathy with the singers. The extensive experience of Marilyn Zschau and Rodney Macann made her wilful Salome and his proud Jokanaan totally credible, the living legend Heather Begg sang for the first time with State Opera as Herodias and Christopher Doig made his role debut with the horrid Herod. Thomas Edmonds had announced prior to the opening that Narraboth would be his last role in opera. When hopeless love for the wilful adolescent Salome made him fall on his sword ten minutes in, many wondered why he should regard his death as terminal. Doubtless he had his reasons, but loss of vocal tone and power could not have been among them. Over a period of nearly thirty years he had sung roles by de Falla, Ravel, Janáček, Donizetti, and Puccini, all with considerable acclaim, in 35 separate productions with IOG, NOSA and SOSA. But his most admired work was for Mozart – Tamino in *The Magic Flute* in 1983 and Don Ottavio in *Don Giovanni* in 1985. Anyone who has heard Edmonds complete the long melisma in *Il mio tesoro* and glide into the following reprise without taking a breath measures all other tenors by him.

It is fitting that this chapter should end with his retirement.

12

Company-in-Waiting –

1995–97

⁂

Nineteen ninety-five began auspiciously for State Opera in March with 20,000 attending Opera in the Park, a concert of excerpts from the coming season. In *La Bohème* in May, the main lovers, Judith Henley (Mimi) and Antonio Adame, were overshadowed by Marcello (Douglas McNicol), Matthew Henrick (Schaunard) and David Hibbard (Colline), all three of them young, enormously endearing, naturally endowed with fine voices and developing before your eyes in vocal and theatrical technique.

Several times since the appointment of Bill Gillespie as chief executive mention had been made of the growing 'internationalisation' of the company, in the form of sharing productions and engaging outstanding soloists from outside the country. On May 19 came the astonishing announcement that our company – not the national one in Sydney, not the next in line in Melbourne, but the least likely to stake its claim to membership of opera's international club – was to mount *Der Ring des Nigelungen*. Not until 1998, because such a huge enterprise would take literally years of planning. By August Bill Gillespie had relinquished the day-to-day running of the company to devote all his energies to the job of Artistic Director of the Wagner epic and Stephen Phillips had been elevated from his assistant position to become SOSA's General Director. The *Ring* announcement was greeted with great excitement, considerable scepticism that such a little company could bring off such a huge undertaking, not a little antagonism, and even some relief. In Melbourne on the day the news broke, Donald McDonald, General Manager of The Australian Opera, expressed his pleasure that Adelaide had let his company and the Melbourne one off the hook of feeling obliged to mount opera's most famous and most notorious cycle. The full story of the preparation and fruition of *The Ring* is told in the ensuing chapter.

In the meantime State Opera had its business-as-usual to attend to. After six years of mainly re-cycled productions, a brand-new one, especially of Verdi's masterly *Falstaff*, was cause for celebration. Not entirely unalloyed, however, because it came at a cost not to be measured in money. As a result of agreements between the regional opera companies and the Australia Council, funds were made available through the Opera Conference, an alliance of the senior executives from around the country, for one special production each year to be built and given its première in each capital city in turn, and then toured nationally. *Eugene Onegin* was the first of these and *Falstaff* the second. Director Simon Phillips, previously with the State Theatre Company, brought fellow New Zealander Iain Aitken to create a set not only functional and witty (in the market villagers shopped at Ford's Fruit and Page's Poultry) but also giving the singers a decent chance to be heard by enclosing all the action in an acoustic shell. All benefited, including Malcolm Donnelly, a robust and rambunctious Falstaff whose belief in his own irresistible way with the ladies – who would not adore that gorgeous booming bass? – was entirely credible. Tracey Grant dressed the principal women, led by Marilyn Richardson as Alice Ford, in shades of green, graduating from jade to pastels, and the chorus in stone to match the Tudor buildings. In equally good taste was John de Main's management of the score. The thrill of witnessing a splendid, spanking bright, totally fresh production was somewhat tempered by the knowledge that such luxuries were to be enjoyed but once a year, and then not until the Opera Conference scheme was fully operational. And of course our turn for the première would only come around once in five years. Concern was quite widespread that designers and directors would be severely restricted in opportunities to start from scratch, the inevitable result that many were likely to seek work outside Australia. For singers, the policy was a mixed blessing – it would impose limits on the available roles, but also allow some of those who shone to repeat their characters in up to five seasons in different cities, thereby establishing highly desirable specialisations.

Also determined to put an individual stamp on his Festival, Barry Kosky followed Christopher Hunt's lead when mounting the 1996 Adelaide Festival of Arts, arguing that no one would miss a major modern opera because so many of his shows were music theatre pieces anyway. He was wrong, and the omission was widely observed and criticised with some heat, though there was some compensation in TAO's Ozopera *Magic Flute*, played in the extremely dilapidated Queen's Theatre, built in 1841 and Australia's oldest remaining mainland theatre. State Opera's share in this Festival was limited to a semi-staging of Gershwin's *Blue Monday* and *Trouble in Tahiti* by Bernstein in the Adelaide Town Hall, a venue not particuarly conducive to the creation of a theatrical atmosphere. Dobbs Franks conducted the Adelaide Symphony Orchestra, getting a reasonably up-beat result from them and lead singers Kirsti Harms, Grant Doyle and David Lemke.

Victoria State Opera's sets and costumes for *Les Pêcheurs de Perles* was looking every minute of its age – ten years – when brought to Adelaide to open the 1996 season. Marilyn Richardson's first venture into direction did not persuade her away from her main career as a greatly admired singing actress, but Douglas McNicol (Zurga) and Patrick Power (Nadir) both added to their already substantial reputations. McNicol's success with Bizet's original *tessitura* encouraged him to extend his range and hence enhance his employability. It also helped him win a Churchill Fellowship which took him overseas for further studies to stabilise those crucial extra three semitones. The local press was much taken with conductor David Stanhope, not only for his Bizet but for his collaboration with composer Nigel Westlake on the score for the film *Babe*, which to their utter astonishment became a national and international triumph.

One of the few operas with a totally credible plot and almost universally loved music, *Eugene Onegin* was another Opera Conference venture. Choeographer Garth Welch worked a dancer's magic on the chorus, cajoling them into convincing peasant dances and imbuing them with a rare sense of purpose, all the more commendable because they were singing in Russian. Prudence Dunstone (Olga) and Claire Primrose (Tatyana) made significant role debuts and Greg Tomlinson gave one of his most outstanding interpretations with a highly charged Lensky. At his peak in the poignant aria delivered in full knowledge that he will die the next day in a duel brought on by his challenge to Onegin over a trivial flirtation with Lensky's fiancée, he held the audience in thrall, lamenting with him that a girl's thoughtlessness and his own stupid pride could bring his life to a futile end.

The proximity of operas within a season can sometimes enhance their dramatic impact. By following *Onegin* with *Don Pasquale* (Opera Conference again) a few months later the company emphasised both the seriousness of the one and the frivolity of the other. In close-up in Her Majesty's Theatre, the details of Donizetti's sometimes distinctly unfunny comedy had immediate impact, and Conal Coad and Amelia Farrugia delivered the lascivious old miser and his scheming hussy of a wife right into our laps. A piffling error in rehearsal grew, as can happen, into a wonderfully funny bit of business for cast, conductor, orchestra and audience. The Don, reading a letter, mispronounces 'sa' instead of 'fa'. Graham Abbott corrects him. The Don takes offence and glares ferociously. Keep it in, says the director. Next time, the Don says (with Italian accent) 'Non, is sa.' Conductor – 'Non, is fa' and points his baton to the score in confirmation. Next time, Abbott shows the score to the audience sitting at his heels. Then to the orchestra. After Adelaide, *Pasquale* played in Brisbane. By that time the orchestra was joining in to back the conductor. 'Non, is fa' they chorused. After 15 performances, the joke was wearing a bit thin, but Abbott still loves the story. Later in the year Timothy Sexton conducted *Pasquale* on tour, with David Hibbard taking the lead role.

AO AND VSO TO BECOME ONE FROM 1998, shouted the headlines of the national journal *Opera Australasia* in November 1996. In a coup that took even the best informed opera buffs around the country completely unawares, on 7 October the two companies announced that they had agreed to merge. Actually the result was more of a takeover by Sydney of Melbourne than a merger, and despite all the assurances by the chairmen of both the eastern companies SOSA's antenna were quickly on full alert lest their greedy eyes turned to Adelaide, Perth and Brisbane in the hope of gobbling them up as well. Part of the deal with the Victorian government entailed having a brand new name for the combined company, initially named Australian National Opera. When singers literate in Italian pointed out that the initials translate to 'arse' in one of opera's most used languages, the brand became Opera Australia. Hold on, said members of the National Council meeting in Sydney, that's the name of the country's opera journal. Too bad – the journal's name had not been registered nationally, and it lost out. Swallowing his bitter resentment at this cavalier treatment, the journal's editor and founder David Gyger took out world registration for *Opera-Opera*, and explained why in a typically oblique article entitled 'The Minnow and the Whale' (*Opera Australasia*, January 1997).

Back in Adelaide, as recorded in the 1997 Annual Report, regular turnover of Board members brought in Adelaide jeweller Albert Bensimon, Robert Pontifex and Deborah Morgan from the business sector, and Lillian Scott, a previous chair of the Friends. The name of Diana Ramsay was added to the list of Life Members in recognition of her generosity, most notably in her sponsorship of the surtitles which had been crucial in helping to debunk much of the mystery (without in the least diminishing the magic) of opera. In his first report to the Minister of Arts Diana Laidlaw, Chairman Timothy O'Loughlin made special mention of the loss of Life Member and Board member Doris Brokensha who had died in November 1996, commending her contribution to the development of opera and young artists in this state, and her long association with the Friends of State Opera.

Opera companies everywhere have *The Marriage of Figaro* near the top of their agendas. It is Mozart, it is funny and sad, it deals with matters of universal and timeless import and will remain in fashion as long as people in power try to browbeat those subservient to them. It attracts patrons over and over again, happy to see new productions, or to admire for the umpteenth time old ones – like John Copley's for The Australian Opera, first aired in 1971 and still looking good 26 years on – and new singers with different angles on the characters so perceptively crafted by the composer and his librettist Lorenzo da Ponte. In 1997 State Opera followed its 1978 example and the 'baby' Figaro of 1990 with Copley's authentic and elegant view. There was plenty for the most seasoned *Figaro* collectors to admire in Kate Ladner's ingenue-cum-wordly wise Susanna and Ghillian Sullivan's coquette-cum-Countess, and a splendid surprise when Geoffrey Harris managed to make a star turn out of a minor character, Basilio the music teacher. As proof of a genuine comic gift, the more unobtrusive he tried to be the more he was noticed.

The last opera to be staged before *Der Ring* totally appropriated State Opera's energies was Gale Edwards's Opera Conference production of Puccini's *Manon Lescaut*, of major interest to patrons who had seen Massenet's *Manon*, basically the same story, in 1985. Several crucial roles were unconvincingly cast, but the stylish and committed conducting of Richard Bonynge was full of the character that was often missing on stage.

To appease those patrons who were distinctly displeased that for 1998 it was Wagner or nothing, in May State Opera mounted an extremely successful double bill of Stravinsky's *Mavra* and Vaughan Williams's *Riders to the Sea* in the Opera Studio, part of the recently acquired company premises in the western suburbs of Adelaide. Singers whose voices and personalities were swamped in the 2,000 seater Festival Theatre bloomed before 200 spectators, and the pairing of a wickedly funny farce (Brian Gilbertson disguising his hairy Hussar legs in the black plastic skirt and frilly apron of a French maid) with John Millington Synge's harrowing picture of Maurya – Wendy Hopkins – losing all her six sons to the insatiable maw of the sea with heart-rending resignation increased the impact of both. Director Catherine Carter and designer Gaelle Mellis brought an extra measure of verisimilitude to the Vaughan Williams by covering the stage with fresh, still tangy seaweed.

Thanks to the management skills and diplomacy of Bill Gillespie and Stephen Phillips, by the time the previous two chapters in the company's history closed, the disaster with which they had opened was theoretically over, but never to be forgotten.

In August 1998 veteran supporter and promoter Kathleen Steele Scott died after a short illness. Almost to her last breath, spent quite by chance reminiscing with IOG baritone Powell Harrison over a brandy and soda, she revelled in her forty years of association with Intimate Opera Group, New Opera South Australia and The State Opera of South Australia, and her one regret in dying was that she would miss *Der Ring des Nibelungen*.

13

With this Ring – 1998

⚜

Der Ring des Nibelungen in Adelaide? Put on by the State Opera? When Premier Dean Brown announced on 19 May 1995 that this monumental opera cycle was to be mounted by a regional company after an attempt by The Australian Opera had been abandoned halfway through and the Victoria State Opera had never got past the initial planning stage, amazement, even disbelief was a common reaction from the eastern states. For Adelaide, it was a moment of triumphant glee.

This would not be the first performance of the cycle in Australia – Irish impresario Thomas Quinlan brought a European production to Melbourne and Sydney in 1913, but ours would be the first using substantially Australian soloists, chorus and orchestra, as well as technical staff and crew. The story of how it all came about is almost as bizarre as Wagner's plot.

Since 1983, Adelaide had played host to the final race of the Formula 1 Grand Prix car race. It was a good money spinner for the government because it attracted large numbers of tourists to the city. After 11 years, the race was wooed to Melbourne by Victorian Premier Jeff Kennett in spite of expressions of outrage and accusations of treachery from South Australia. Australian Major

Cast photo, *The Ring*, 1998

Events (AME), a state instrumentality charged with the responsibility of initiating and organising large scale shows of all types, invited the performing arts companies (among many others) to submit proposals for large popular spectacles in which the government might invest for a decent return, and incidentally soothe the wounded pride of the bureaucrats and politicians who felt that they had been cheated out of the Grand Prix.

The response of Bill Gillespie and Stephen Phillips of SOSA was unhesitating. With the support of Len Amadio, *The Ring*, they said to SOSA chairman

Timothy O'Loughlin, was the only possible choice. It would bring Wagner aficionados from all over Australia and overseas to see the first modern staging of the epic in our country–these people would be mainly affluent and would stay in superior accommodation and eat in the best restaurants, as well as visiting the wineries and other local tourist attractions. Given a preliminary green light, the instigators decided that a completely new production was out of the question in terms of both time and money, and Gillespie set out to visit established but still fresh productions in Europe and the USA.

His recommendation was to bring Pierre Strosser's creation from the Théâtre du Châtelet in Paris. It had been shown in only one season in 1994, it had been well received by critics – with some reservations – and the public, and was reasonably transportable. Budgeting proceeded with government approval, and once it was calculated that there would be a handsome return on the investment of public money, and that the generosity of sponsors could be depended on because of the magnitude of the project, the decision was made to proceed. The cost of the whole enterprise was estimated at $8 million, and it was anticipated that between $10 million and $15 million would be spent in SA, over and above the ticket prices, on accommodation, travel, restaurants, galleries and shops. Within a few months the Châtelet management, Strosser and the English conductor Jeffrey Tate were signed, a Ring Corporation was set up with prominent opera identity Donald McDonald as its chairman, Bill Gillespie resigned as General Director of SOSA to become Artistic Director of *The Ring* and Stephen Phillips took over the company's top job as well as that of the project's General Manager.

Reactions were mixed, but on balance favourable. The local Wagner Society was naturally delighted. SOSA's subscribers were divided into those who genuinely supported the idea, others whose loyalty to the company overcame their reservations and the rest, who disliked Wagner intensely and decided early on that they would have none of it. Some changed their minds when the event was actually on the stage, but only about a quarter of them accepted the company's invitation to begin paying for *The Ring* with their 1996 subscriptions and were peeved to find that there would be no other opera in 1998. But there was no turning back. The State Government had pledged support, the Ring Corporation set its own target to be raised through private sponsorship, and the date was set for November 1998. The four operas would be played, in the order and timetable Wagner intended for them, namely *Das Rheingold* day one, *Die Valkyrie* day two, *Siegfried* day four and *Götterdämmerung* day seven, and the whole cycle would be run three times. SOSA was aiming for a total audience of about 6,000.

The Adelaide Symphony Orchestra's 80 players fell short of Wagner's ideals – in the Bayreuth Festival Theatre, where the operas were first performed in 1876 and are still being aired every July and August, the first three have 120 players and the last 132 – so an extra 40 players had to be found, most of them from outside the state, as well as the special Wagner tubas. Casting presented a further raft of problems. In the whole world at any one time there are only a handful of singers with the range, power and timbre capable of meeting Wagner's demands for the main characters at an international standard, and they are often booked up years in advance. To Australia's great credit, only six of the most prominent roles had to be imported – all the rest of the 27 principals were from Australia and New Zealand. Then there was the matter of the acoustics in the Adelaide Festival Theatre (AFT), the only possible venue in Adelaide for such a huge enterprise. Ever since it was opened in 1973, musicians, audiences and critics (especially critics) had been complaining about its lack of resonance, and all concerned realised that drastic action was needed to satisfy the expectations of visitors who would have heard *The Ring* in some of the world's most ideal acoustics – Bayreuth, in particular – as well as local patrons. SOSA was a prime mover in persuading the government to pay for major refurbishment, removing the carpet and replacing the seats. Further, experts were called in to advise on a sound system that would do justice to the performers. The Lexicon Acoustic Resonance Enhancement System (LARES) was duly selected and installed. The total cost of the refurbishment and LARES was estimated at $1 million.

In Paris, the set was packed into ten forty-foot containers and shipped to Adelaide. It all arrived to great excitement and extensive press coverage. The basic sloping platform that provided the raked floor was assembled at SOSA's rehearsal studios at Netley and by early August most of the singers, the director and his assistants and the musical director and assistants had arrived. Rehearsals began immediately. Some questions were asked about why three months of rehearsal were necessary for the singers – the Châtelet production was said to be simple, one of the reasons for Gillespie's choice – and why the orchestra should need 200 hours to learn four operas – the normal rate would be one opera per week – but assurances were given that these conditions had been imposed by the director and conductor and were *sine qua non*.

Advance publicity was intense. In September 1997, more than a year before the event, *The Ring* Ancillary Events Committee, chaired by Christine Rothauser, organised a 'Weekend with *The Ring*' for local and interstate subscribers who had already bought their tickets. The event began with a reception at Government House hosted by the Governor, Sir Eric Neal, and Lady Neal. Lectures and panel discussions from singers, directors, engineers, critics, scholars and administrators occupied all day Saturday and Sunday, with *The Ring* Dinner in between.

The Wagner virus (Leo Schofield, speaker at the Weekend dinner, planted the term) spread rapidly through the community. The Wagner Society planned meetings, the Musicological Society organised a conference on 'Wagner at the Millennium' with a number of prominent international Wagner scholars as speakers, exhibitions were set in train for the Art Gallery, the Festival Theatre Foyer, the Adelaide Town Hall and other venues, tours were organised to entice visitors to extend their stay in South Australia, two local writers put together and produced plays about Wagner, a book was written about the cycle by local enthusiast Peter Bassett and introductory lectures were scheduled to take place before each of the twelve performances.

Patrons were warned that bodily comfort was essential and advised to get a good pair of Wagner shoes to allow their leg and foot muscles to relax while seated and to take them on refreshing walks through the neighbouring Elder Park and along the banks of the River Torrens during the long intervals. Plays on words flowed from the press like the Rhine. 'Opera buffs run rings around petrol heads'; 'Grand Prix goes East, but Adelaide revs up for Wagner's Ring'; 'Ring cycle an opera Grand Prix'; 'Cycle predicted to ring in $14 m for State coffers'; 'A Ring of confidence'; 'Lord of The Ring;' and many many more.

The publicity paid off. Although the prices, $950 down to $450, plus $45 for a glossy program comprising articles by local and overseas writers and greetings from the Premier, John Olsen and the Minister for the Arts, Diana Laidlaw, were steep by Adelaide standards, the seats were about 85 per cent booked in advance, roughly half from interstate and a quarter each from South Australia and overseas. The cycle has a huge cult following; large numbers of fans track all over the world, notching up *Rings* in their diaries, spending large sums of money on travel and tickets, often meeting up with each other in Seattle, Vienna, Munich and New York, and now, for the first time ever, in Adelaide, South Australia. A large contingent from the USA included one devotee who was seeing his fiftieth *Ring*. According to reports, he held court in his hotel room each night after performances, and was sought after by the media for his views on 'Our *Ring*'.

Generally the response from the audiences was wildly enthusiastic, even verging on the hysterical. Although some among them were *Ring* collectors, many were novices, not only new to the epic, but also, judging by the numbers who flashed cameras during the performances, unfamiliar with the conventions of behaviour in the theatre. The majority, especially the SOSA regulars who had supported their company out of loyalty as much as from devotion to Wagner, were caught up in the surge of excitement that seemed to pervade the whole city, and declared that they had got their money's worth. At roughly a dollar a minute.

The list of overseas and Australian media attending ran to more than fifty names reporting to print, radio and television outlets ranging from London's *Opera* magazine and *The Times* to *Vogue* and *Vanity Fair*. All major Australian daily newspapers sent journalists. Most of the country's opera critics came. Some writers were positively euphoric about the production, the singing, the acting, the orchestra, the theatre, the weather, the wine, Adelaide and the whole spectacle. Never had SOSA been the subject of such a barrage of publicity and such a plethora of praise. Fortunately the excesses were tempered by a number of reviews by regular opera critics, most of them Australian, whose direct, live experience of some of the most highly regarded *Rings* of recent years equipped them to make properly substantiated judgements of this one.

David Gyger (*Opera-Opera*, December 1998) noted the atmosphere in Adelaide before the opening of 'self-congratulatory exuberance and artistic trepidation', and deemed the exercise 'a qualified triumph – a nearly unmitigated one for the enlarged Adelaide Symphony Orchestra and conductor Jeffrey Tate, a very intermittent one for director/designer Pierre Strosser and a modified one for the team of soloists.' Michael Henderson sat on the fence, telling his readers (*Spectator*, 2 January 1999) that 'To some seasoned Wagnerians' Pierre Strosser's production 'was banal'. Other critics approved of the bare stage and limited movement, finding 'a poetic transparency that worked, at times triumphantly'. The most extensive and most perceptive account came from Paul Thomason (*Opera News*, July 1999). His 'Letter from Adelaide' singled out for special praise Daniel Sumegi (Hagen), Warwick Fyfe

(Fasolt) and Liane Keegan (Erda) and found five of the most prominent characters 'disappointing'. Thomason was unequivocally critical of the production. 'Strosser's direction ... ran counter to Wagner's wishes at every opportunity.' He described the one and only moment of real drama in the whole four operas thus. 'The production's one *coup de théâtre* came in *Rheingold* when, instead of the rainbow bridge, a giant black monolith erupted from under the stage, like the back end of a submarine emerging from the ocean, splintering the floor with a resounding crack and bisecting the entire stage.' Strosser is quoted as saying 'It means whatever you want it to mean'. Thomason responded with 'What it meant to most people who knew the *Ring* was Strosser's utter perversity and poverty of imagination. The list of such perversions was endless.' The critic was positively fulsome in his accolades for Jeffrey Tate's 'inspired leadership' and the 'almost tactile sense of beauty' in the playing of the Adelaide Symphony Orchestra. Thomason makes some references to the LARES but apparently did not appreciate that two microphones above the pit and four more above the stage plus 257 speakers around the stage and auditorium had a considerable effect on the orchestra's volume and resonance as well as on the clarity of individual instruments.

In the aftermath, all concerned basked in the compliments, whatever their origin, and even the sceptics who said it would never happen and did not subscribe (though many of them eventually bought single tickets, and even more crowded in to the Playhouse to watch free transmissions on the huge TV screen from the Festival Theatre next door) could not escape feeling pride in the accomplishment. As Stephen Phillips told *Opera-Opera* (May 1999), 'This was the first time that State Opera had been asked to market anything outside Adelaide. It's the first time in music theatre in Australia that a single production has been marketed both nationally and internationally.'

Whatever anyone, expert or tyro, thought of the work, the production and the musical standards of the whole enterprise, there can be no argument about the credit due to the staff of State Opera and to the support they engendered from both state and federal governments in bringing this monument of music theatre to fruition in Adelaide. The reputation of the company was immeasurably enhanced and at least some of the sceptics were confounded.

No sooner had the last echoes of Siegfried's funeral march floated away across the Torrens than there was talk of another *Ring* for Adelaide, this time a homegrown production. During 1999 an extensive national enquiry into funding Australia's major companies was carried out. The outcome was increased ongoing federal grants for nearly all of them, including SOSA and ASO, and a special $1 million to the former for another *Ring* in 2004.

The Adelaide Critics Circle gave Bill Gillespie a Special Award in December 1998 just after he had been appointed director of the Western Australian Academy of the Performing Arts. In part the citation reads:

> His crowning operatic glory is also South Australia's. His was the idea of doing *The Ring*, his the proposal to bring the production from the Châtelet, his primarily the responsibility of casting the roles, of fixing the orchestra, of ensuring that everything worked to the best possible advantage ... Arguments over the pros and cons of the Strosser-Tate *Ring* will rage for at least the foreseeable future. No one can deny the benefits the singers, the supers, the orchestra, the critics, the audiences (many of them instant *Ring* experts) have gained through the huge extension of our operatic horizon as that has taken place over the three weeks of the *Ring*. This award expresses the gratitude of the Adelaide Critics Circle for the part Bill Gillespie has played in elevating the operatic sophistication of our state.

14

One Grail Leads to Another –

1999–2000

❧

Whatever the verdict on the artistic value of the Châtelet *Ring*, conquering the opera world's Everest had vastly enhanced State Opera's reputation nationally and internationally.

Within South Australia, the company had a job of work to do with its subscribers. Aiming to win back substantial numbers who had turned their backs on Wagner, the 1999 program promised a broadly based selection of popular pieces. But the offended ones were not to be wooed so easily. Many complained that Gilbert and Sullivan's *The Mikado* was *infra dig* for a professional opera company and some (probably those who had turned up their noses at *Countess Maritza* and *The Czardas Princess*) were equally snitchy about the flighty *Fledermaus* (this time around without its definite article). *Butterfly* and *Trovatore* were of course thoroughly respectable, but the courageous little geisha had disembowelled herself in four previous productions and the gypsy had thrown the wrong baby on the fire in one. Was there nothing new?

Stephen Phillips, just a tad put out that choices intended to placate his patrons had instead inflamed them, stuck to his guns. *Butterfly* was coming in a different guise, directed by Moffatt Oxenbould and getting rapturous reviews in Sydney, and the dreadful war that divided the Spanish nation and its families in the fifteenth century would be re-set into the Spanish Civil War of 1936 in a new production by Elke Neidhardt, jointly funded by the regional companies of SA, Queensland and Western Australia. So there. The relative affluence of the company – posting a surplus of $95,000 in the previous year – allowed it to offer four operas in 1999.

As Phillips had hoped, *Fledermaus* was a magnet for the general public, and most of the regulars turned up too – a bit grudgingly, some of them, but loyalty required their presence. The press was subjected to a tasteless, crass pre-publicity stunt. Invitations were distributed to a gathering in the Presidential Suite (of the Stamford Plaza) promising 'More Scandals than the White House' and interviews with Miss Monica Lewinsky and Mr Kenneth Starr. When critics, reporters and broadcasters arrived they were greeted by a monstrous, cross-dressed caricature of the notorious aide and a lookalike prosecutor. Cashing in on current scandals such as the President and the intern is one thing. It might have seemed like a good idea at the time, but fell flat on its over-painted face and unbelievable bosom.

Misguided also was director Lindy Hume's decision to transplant the setting from 1890 Vienna to 1930 New York. It all looked quite gorgeous, and a mainly splendid cast – Ghillian Sullivan (Rosalinde), Grant Smith (Gabriel), Douglas McNicol (Dr Falke), Amelia Farrugia (Adele), Kirsti Harms (Orlovsky) and Paul Blackwell, exquisitely funny in several non-singing roles – carried off the Americanisms with aplomb. But no amount of upper-class New York accent could atone for the contradiction between the scenery and the score – two halves, each of a different show, was the verdict.

Also highly critical was the judgement passed on the LARES system installed in time for the *Ring* cycle in the previous year and in use with an opera for the first time since then. Complaints about its application to Wagner were as nought compared with the mayhem that was perpetrated against Strauss on opening night. Offensive volume levels from the orchestra were bad enough. Voices came at the audience from all angles, familiar ones, especially the women, taking on some very strange hues. Worst of all, the singers were fitted with personal microphones which were centrally controlled and intended only for the spoken dialogue. Tacky fingered technicians were blamed for the sudden surges and ebbings that preceded and followed many of the speeches. Several enraged letters were sent to the management and courteous disclaimers were received. Anecdotal evidence suggests that matters were toned down later in the season, but LARES had failed dismally in its first post-*Ring* test.

Heed was taken. Elke Neidhardt came to Adelaide fresh from a very heated and very public disagreement with the conductor over the staging in her production of *Tannhäuser* in Sydney, and was expected to ensure that nothing, including a far from perfect amplification system, would stand between her and her determination to get the very best visual and aural outcome for her *Trovatore*. Michael Scott-Mitchell's bombed-out shell gave shelter to all who needed it and also projected the voices so well that LARES was set at the lowest spot on its opera dial – Stephen Phillips had obviously taken charge and said that if it was any lower it would be off.

Discussion on the rights of a director to take such extensive liberties were lively and frequently unusually intelligent, ranging well beyond the shallow grounds on which preferences are commonly based. A few traditionalists objected to Judith Hoddinott's 1930s underwear and negligées and two of Adelaide's senior critics, Tristram Cary (*Australian*, 16 August, pro) and Roger Knight (*Adelaide Review*, September, con) were diametrically opposed in their assessment. No one seemed too worried when the new recruits bared their bottoms to the audience while exchanging their gypsy rags for Republican uniforms – at the last performance the cheeky lads tied bits of tinsel and other decorations where they would attract the most attention, testing the sangfroid of the military inspectors who had to face the audience and giving the press a titillating story.

Il trovatore won for State Opera the Adelaide Critics Circle award for the 1999 Best Performing Arts Company.

In repertory with *Trovatore* was *The Mikado*, presented by arrangement with OA. Tim Goodchild's totally Nipponised sets and costumes embraced the predominantly young cast, giving them multiple possibilities for funny business and they grasped every one – occasionally with an excess of fervour. Timothy Sexton conducted the custom-built South Australian Light Opera Orchestra.

The success of the 1998 double bill encouraged the company to repeat the exercise. Scott Joplin's dramatically obfuscated and musically not particularly entertaining *Treemonisha* had to rely on academic interest for its acceptance, whereas the interpretation of *Mahagonny Songspiel* from Catherine Carter and her designer Gaelle Mellis did them, Kurt Weill and Berthold Brecht and the company proud.

Moffatt Oxenbould's *Madama Butterfly* captured the essence of this delicate creature as none of the previous airings (1983, 1987, 1991 and 1993, the last in outdoor concert form) had done. The complete production crew – Vladimir Kamirski (Conductor), Matthew Barclay (Assistant Director and Choreography), Russell Cohen and Peter England (design) and Robert Bryan (Lighting Designer) were brought in from Sydney, and Oxenbould was here to direct the whole thing, thus preserving intact, and even building on, his original vision. 'A production of immense grace and power' was the pithily accurate summary of critic Ewart Shaw (*Advertiser*, 25 October), who added that 'the design team has created a floating world … where simplicity and elegance of appearance mask the sophisticated intelligence and skill of the creators'. Anke Höppner carried her Butterfly with supreme composure from innocence to death and took the audience on the same inexorable journey. Her locally cast family (Sally-Anne Russell as Suzuki, Douglas McNicol as Sharpless) and her betrayer-husband Pinkerton (inspired casting of Greg Tomlinson) and the beautifully deployed chorus and kabuki attendants flew with her. Kamirski held the music together with artistry equal to that of Oxenbould's production.

Government funding, both state and federal, was prominent in arts news throughout 1999. In May State Opera was granted its persistent request to get triennial funding – Bill Gillespie had been urging its advantages for at least seven years – allowing the company to plan with some sense of certainty for the immediate future. The best artists, whether Australians or otherwise, get booked up well in advance, and yearly funding cannot guarantee the standards that audiences had come to expect. Arts professionals all over the whole country had been following with interest the progress of the Nugent Report, a national assessment of the needs of Australia's major organisations conducted by Helen Nugent, an astute businesswoman and a thoughtful arts patron. State Opera was watching very closely, and issued a call to arms at one point over a draft recommendation that they and the Adelaide Symphony Orchestra pool their administrations. Not practicable, said both, as did their counterparts in other states over similar suggestions. But the final outcome was good for opera in our state. The company was designated as 'niche', specialising in unusual repertoire. Actually, that's what we have been doing since IOG in 1957, though admittedly not consistently, was the gratified riposte. The best news was that the federal government would allocate an extra $52 million to the 31 companies under consideration over the next four years, and that SOSA would get a substantial share, including $3 million to stage a second *Ring* in 2004. Nugent succeeded where Paul Keating's 1994 Creative Nation proposals had failed because she eschewed rhetoric and concentrated on proper recognition and remuneration of excellence.

Artistic successes in 1999 were unfortunately not equally productive at the box office, which had dropped by ten per cent below the previous year. One ploy to entice more converts to the world of opera in 2000 was to engage in co-operative events with the ASO and the Festival Centre. Chorus and principals from the company starred, some of them rather too brightly, in *Magnifico*, arguably the best ever of the orchestra's Showtime series. Whether the full and wildly enthusiastic house would turn out again for *Tosca* and *Roméo et Juliette* in full was anybody's guess, and all the evidence so far is that they would not, but the risk was a calculated one.

Writing to Vermeer was a huge risk. Robyn Archer's choice for the centrepiece of her 2000 Adelaide Festival of Arts had no big singing names, the composer was unknown in Australia, the piece was to première in Amsterdam and then come directly to Adelaide and she was gambling on promises rather than proofs. The one name widely recognised was Peter Greenaway, famous or notorious, depending on your attitude, for his films. Whether his name, or the extravagant publicity about the elaborate staging with lots of water and the starring role of a cow called Linda, or the multi-media nature of the piece – which usually means that the audience will not be challenged by unfriendly music – *Vermeer* sold out. Hailed as reviving the tradition of including a major modern opera in the Adelaide Festival of Arts, which it certainly was not, it surpassed even 1998's spectacularly unspectacular Wagner in arguability. The critics led the pack. 'Exhausting and unsatisfying ... deliberately obtuse ... dilettantish appropriation of someone else's art', scoffed John Slavin (*Age*, 7 March). 'An incomparable celebration of turn-of-the century performance art' defended

Roger Knight (*Adelaide Review*, January 2000), who had already seen it in Amsterdam, as had Roger Covell (*Age*, 15 October) who proclaimed it 'one of the most completely realised, masterfully planned productions seen in Europe in a generation'. Even the most disapproving observers agreed on the beauty of the paintings adorning the set, but local writer Peter Goers opined privately and Wilde-ishly that 'there was less to this than meets the eye'. Offstage, obvious arguments between writer Greenaway and director Saskia Boddeke over who deserved the credit for what added spice to the whole occasion. State Opera's share was mundane but crucial – building part of the set, rounding up extras, engaging understudies, providing rehearsal space, auditioning bovine applicants for the key role of Linda, and attending to all matters of organisation and co-ordination with the Festival Centre and the ASO. Not too daunting an assignment for a company that has done *The Ring*.

Così fan tutte was State Opera's coming out (as in debutante) in 1975, marking its emergence into the real, as distinct from the idealistic, world of opera, and the same production, by Anthony Besch and John Stoddart, had returned in 1982 to be admired and enjoyed all over again. State Opera opened its 2000 season with an acclaimed collaboration of the same opera between German Carl Friedrich Oberle and Swedish Goran Jarvefelt, who had died suddenly during rehearsals of the production for The Australian Opera in 1989. During the next decade, their work had entertained audiences in Sydney, Melbourne and Brisbane without losing any of its wit and freshness. In August came Adelaide's turn at The Opera Conference's *Roméo et Juliette*, not Gounod's most famous, nor most effective opera, but making its first appearance in Adelaide. Kate Ladner and Gordon Gietz were well tuned as the lovers following their season in Perth, and among a goodly bunch of local singers essaying their roles anew, veteran bass baritone Robert Dawe brought a wealth of vocal and dramatic maturity to Capulet, his first appearance for State Opera, and his first operatic role since New Opera's *Broucek* in 1974.

A re-run of Michael Blakemore's 1993 *Tosca*, a co-production with Welsh National Opera which had been in the meantime to Houston and back to Wales, was keenly awaited as State Opera's closer for 2000, not for its somewhat cramped set for the church of Sant'Andrea della Valle but because Deborah Riedel was to make her debut as the glamorous opera star. This was a coup for

State Opera, as she had been singing major roles in some of the world's great houses since her *Sandrina's Secret* and *Czardas Princess* here in 1987 – her only appearance in Adelaide since then was in 1991, when she memorably partnered José Carerras in the Entertainment Centre and 10,000 guests joyously accepted their invitation to sing along in the *Brindisi* with them at Violetta's party.

The coup nearly turned into a cancellation. During rehearsals Riedel had been fighting off a bronchial infection. Up to the final dress run, cover Christine Beasley had been standing by. On the Thursday preceding opening night, Riedel was pronounced fit and Beasley flew home to Sydney. On Saturday around 12.30 pm Stephen Phillips took a phone call of the type that opera managers have nightmares about. Riedel had a recurrence of her virus and was unable to perform that night. An SOS to Joan Carden in Sydney got her on a plane (in the last seat left) and in Adelaide, with her own costume (Opera Australia's wardrobe was opened up by special arrangement) by 5.30. The role was fresh in her voice from a recent season in Sydney – but the production was a complete stranger. She met her lover and her would-be rapist and they walked her through Act I. In the first and second intervals, ditto Act II and III. Before curtain up, the General Director gave the performance of his life, milking the story for every drop of drama. Carden had been on the point of taking her dogs for a walk when her phone rang – five minutes later and she would have been out of reach. Her first entrance, after her imperious demands – 'Mario! Mario!' – to be let into the church where he is painting his Madonna brought tumultuous applause. Not the most hawk-eyed could have spotted a moment's hesitation in her moves and business, and she sang her heart out, as Tosca must. In other circumstances Stuart Skelton's velvet-toned Cavaradossi and Daniel Sumegi's entry into the ranks of the villain Scarpia would have taken line honours – as it was, Carden was not only the heroine of the story but also the saviour of the première.

Provocative questions were asked along the lines of 'Is Your Rehearsal Really Necessary?' Roger Knight (*Adelaide Review*, November 2000) suggested that State Opera could 'find their accountants rigorously querying all that time and money spent on rehearsals'. A backstage gossip session worked out that if ten minutes for each of three acts was clearly adequate for *Tosca*, then by that reckoning the whole of *The Ring* could be prepared in 100 minutes.

Deborah Riedel recovered and took the stage for her delayed debut one week later. Understandably she was less florid than ideal for Floria Tosca, but has the capacity to grow into full display of the diva's panoply of temperaments.

State Opera is keenly aware of its obligations to use its facilities and resources for the training of young singers and pianists who show the potential for careers in opera. The Young Artist Development Program was established by Stephen Phillips in 1996, and among those who have benefited are Teresa La Rocca and Grant Doyle, both with feet firmly planted on the middle rungs of the professional ladder. Most appropriately, State Opera's last event for 2000 was a concert by that year's crop of Young Artists, Angela Black, Benjamin Rasheed, Emma Foster, Pelham Andrews and David Thelander. They drew 120 people to cheer them on, and raised $1,100 for one of the most worthy of all causes.

Young artists, from left, Angela Black (soprano), Ben Rasheed (tenor),
Emma Foster (alto), Pelham Andrews (bass) and David Thelander (baritone)

The ideal programming (apart from *Rings* and things) according to General Director Stephen Phillips is to concentrate mainly on the conventional repertoire but to include one unusual, not necessarily modern, opera in each season, thereby keeping the most conservative of his patrons satisfied but also appealing to the adventure seekers. He is supported by an uncommonly strong and diverse Board, including (year 2000) ex-diplomat Peter Bassett, experienced music administrator Patricia Lange and Jeanette Sandford-Morgan, widely known for her fearless and well-informed defence of all things good in music and life. Stephen Phillips's management of the company, especially in regard to the efficiency and involvement of a small – tiny by most standards – full-time staff of only six people, has given State Opera a period of stability that allows it to contemplate mounting another *Ring* with equanimity.

15

Hang On – What About the Chorus?

❧

'It's the chorus you need to talk to', some of them insisted to me at supper after the opening night of *Tosca*, State Opera's and their last hurrah for 2000 and this book. Of course. As everyone knows, a good chorus is the *coeur* of any opera company. Musically and dramatically, and often (though not often enough for them) mentioned in reviews, the chorus can be the pinnacle of a director's real talents (anyone can direct fine principals who can find their way around the set and each other without too much in the way of marching orders) and of the chorus master's (likewise, principals don't need to be taught how to sing). But moving around bunches of amateur singers with limited stage *nous* so they are in the right place at the right time, getting them to impersonate French monks, prostitutes, cigarette factory girls, Russian farmers, Italian nobles, gypsy dancers, Furies from hell, pairs of lovers – very difficult, usually embarrassingly inept – soldiers (lots of soldiers), priests, Gibichung vassals – directors can stand or fall on how well the chorus looks, stands, moves, lies on the floor indulging in an orgy, how they get on and off, while all the time appearing as though they are behaving perfectly naturally. Just as vital in the total production scheme of things is how well the chorus sings. Really expert chorus masters are very rare. Getting the mob to sing from memory the right notes, and in foreign languages (since surtitles were introduced operas have been sung in the original French, German, Italian or Russian), and to blend within and between sections so that no embryo prima donna spoils the fabric of the ensemble requires great skill. To do all this, and to make sure they are aware of what the conductor is doing without standing like zombies and staring at the baton, and comply with a director who wants to scatter them around trees, pillars or statues without considering that they will sound, as well as look, scattered; to get everything as right as possible takes outstanding musical ability, wide experience of stagecraft and enormous tact.

State Opera has been well served by its chorus. A few potential principals have used rank and file positions to learn the works, get practice at being on show and earn funds for their studies. Some have left the chorus to test themselves as soloists and have happily returned to the fold when their aspirations proved to be beyond their capabilities. Most of them have a day job, but take their singing very seriously – more than just a hobby, closer to a second career. Their loyalty to the company is unshakeable, their willingness to learn their scores by heart and attend music and stage rehearsals unlimited, even when it means standing around in the wings or sitting around in the dressing rooms for hours awaiting their calls. And swapping stories and gleaning gossip.

They reckon it's all worth it. They work hard, sometimes with little acknowledgement, but the rewards are many. Their lives are immeasurably enriched by getting up close and personal with great singers like Marilyn Richardson, Thomas Edmonds, Greg Dempsey, Robert Gard, Lauris Elms, June Bronhill, Lyndon Terracini, John Pringle, Yoko Watanabe, Marilyn Zschau, Alberto Remedios; by learning the music trade from such luminaries as Georg Tintner, Myer Fredman, Jonathon Draper, Stuart Challender, Alexander Ingram, David McSkimming, David Kram, David Porcelijn, Jeffrey Tate; by being told to go here, go there, stand still, run away, fight, fornicate, by eminent directors Anthony Besch, Gale Edwards, David Pountney, Dennis Olsen; by seeing Robyn Archer in her first serious music theatre role in 1974 and watching her astonishing rise to world-wide fame over the next two decades.

All of them have had some of the above, and a few have had it all. Robert Angove started in the chorus of *Count Ory* for New Opera in 1973, Rodney

Kirk's first show was *Broucek* in the following year and both were still going with *Tosca* in 2000. Alexander Lizogubow has covered much the same territory apart from some years interstate. John Greene was the baritone in the quartet of singers making up the nucleus of New Opera in 1973 and has floated between chorus and cameo solo roles since then, up to and including *Tosca* in 2000. Money was not their object. Initially they were not paid at all, then later collected $2 per call – petrol money, that's all – but in 1976 a special rate was struck for them. Currently, they get a reasonable deal – less than professional musicians, much more than mere petrol money.

Think of just about any day job – teacher, furniture maker, statistician, butcher, funeral director, engineer, banker, minister of religion, social worker, engineer, sperm donor, hospital porter – someone in the State Opera chorus will be doing it.

They have long and vivid memories, these people, and not only for the operas they have sung and the splendid – and not so splendid – artists they have known. They are great gossips and great story tellers, and could write their own chapter – nay, their own book – about what goes on on and offstage. The following anecdotes have not been subject to any verification or to any censorship, and should be taken as they were given, in a spirit of making sure that this book tells the whole story from all angles, especially that of the chorus. They were taken down verbatim from stayers Robert Angove, Rodney Kirk, David Perry and Lyndon Piddington at a story swapping session lasting nearly five hours in November 2000 and from other sources who volunteered their most savoury memories specifically for this book.

They are not angels, though sometimes they sing like the heavenly host, and confessions about playing up on and offstage are common. For the opening of *Count Ory* the chorus sat in the boxes at the Festival Theatre overlooking the stage with little to do but drink bubbly. At interval the stage manager realised his error and gave them water, but Act II, according to an ear witness, was rather raucous. During meal breaks in *Trovatore* they would all troop next door to the pub where on one occasion refreshments were taken rather too liberally. A soprano lost her balance and fell into a flowerpot, and when the wine jug was being passed during the second act there was not much acting going on; the Anvil Chorus was somewhat loose that night. Pinching morsels of Turkish delight off the tray after each performance of *Italian Girl in Algiers* got out of hand, leaving the soprano one night with no sweetmeats to offer her master. Some Stage Managers are slow learners, it appears.

But it was not only the chorus who were inclined to high jinks. A noted soprano principal took great delight in taunting two of her attendants while she was facing upstage and they were fronting to the audiences. They fought to maintain stiff upper lips while she uttered, sotto voce so only they could hear, comments calculated to disrupt their composure. They could have complained to the Stage Manager, but it became a battle of wills, and they won. In another opera, they were so offended by a director who physically pushed and shoved them into position and called them bloody idiots that they did complain. Unfortunately the Stage Manager could not help; he had suffered exactly the same treatment, and the same label. The chorus had no comeback to a conductor who told them 'When this opera was written, the chorus couldn't read music. I see the situation hasn't changed', but they hated to be underrated. Two men, quite competent musicians, were selected to simulate the Anvil Chorus accompaniment on stage and were given a plastic anvil to hammer while members of the company's music staff played the real thing in the wings. Not being allowed to show their talents was insult enough, but when the real clanging got out of kilter, the pretenders got the blame from the conductor. They were incensed.

Some of their proudest recollections were of occasions when they were able to cover up for mistakes by their superiors. Once when sent on too early in *The Flying Dutchman* they obligingly sang through the overture, to the raised eyebrows of the conductor, then without a twitch, and as one, all forty of them sang it all over again. One baritone vows that had he not inspected the asparagus supper served to Macheath on the night before he was to hang, they both would have got terrible food poisoning because a lazy tech had left it there all weekend. In summer. And they'll never forget the night when a famous actor more accustomed to television than to live audiences got terrible stage fright on his opening night and adlibbed through most of the seven verses of his first song. The chorus, expecting to copy his text, made what sense they could from his example, but by verse three had recovered their sangfroid and took up the proper text. They still believe their self-control helped the lead to recover his.

Accidents happened, some funny, some quite serious. During *Faust*, fake snow – actually confetti – floated from the flies straight into the mouth of the dying tenor Valentin. His aria ended early, but he was not carried off until the right time. A bundle of clothing chucked around on stage in the *Threepenny Opera* bounced into the pit and broke the clarinettist's mouth piece. He finished the opera on his saxophone. Feeling the clasp of his exotic, heavily decorated belt coming undone during a very quiet and emotionally charged scene one of the *Pearl Fisher*'s slaves just had to let it slide until it crashed to the floor with all its jingles jangling. Not me, he dissembled, but his bright red face gave him away.

Theatre people are highly superstitious about both the play and the opera of *Macbeth*, believing the story to be accursed, and State Opera's had more than its share of bad luck with three chorus men suffering serious injury. During a fight scene, a tenor slipped on a spear and strained a groin muscle; running off a dark ramp on stage, a baritone mistook a black curtain for a wall – his spear ripped the material from top to bottom breaking his fall, but he still landed on his back two metres below. Fortunately one of Adelaide's best surgeons was at hand to diagnose a broken coccyx and supervise his recovery; in another fall, a soldier did terrible damage to his shoulder, necessitating extensive reconstruction surgery.

Sometimes the chorus is hardly off stage, woven into the plot so closely that they know exactly what's going on. Not in *Capriccio*. Eight gentlemen of the household of the beautiful Countess Madeleine are required to stand stock still for 45 minutes, moving nothing but their eyes, before singing a lovely double quartet almost at the end of the opera. One obedient servant seemed to feel all over again the actual pain of the effort when recounting the story – one nearly fainted, he remembered. Watching the audience falling asleep did not help. Most of them had no more idea of that was going on than did the gentlemen.

Choruses spend a lot of time standing around, giving them plenty of time to observe – to spy, if we're frank – without being observed. So they become aware of principals who get a bit too enthusiastic with their love partners, conductors who pay closer attention to the dancing girls on stage than to the score, and directors who believe that hands-on is the best way to show the girls and boys of the chorus what is wanted of them. Some of the spy stories are unfortunately unprintable, but one of the best involved a very straightforward tenor who had to ask the Stage Manager to stop a rehearsal in mid-aria. Taking him to one side, he confessed that he simply could not concentrate on his lines while a gaggle of nubile girls in shorts and singlets danced and pranced around him. They were instructed to wear suitably restraining attire.

There to do their bit for the best possible outcome, the chorus never refuse a reasonable request. Costume designer Laurence Blake once called the men's chorus for a costume parade. Sternly he instructed them 'Gentlemen, these trousers have been carefully designed for you to dress to the left. Please make the appropriate adjustments.' During an interval in *Samson et Dalila* the director Lindy Hume called the men's chorus into the rehearsal room, leapt up on a table and berated them soundly for behaving too realistically in the orgy. Donald Beard, six feet five inches of walk-on Philistine, Sturt cricketer and eminent surgeon, says he quaked in his shoes at her fury, but still thinks it unfair that she did not itemise the complaint nor reveal who had made it. Told this story, one of the orgy-makers recalled that some toe-sucking was going on, though he did not find it unseemly. And that was years before this form of foreplay became known as a sport fit for a duchess.

Patrons will always express and exchange opinions as they exit from an opera. Often their views on the principals, the set, the direction, the con-ducting will differ, sometimes quite markedly – even with heat. For the chorus, especially since the radical surgery performed on the Adelaide Festival Theatre's acoustics in 1998 allows their voices to be heard loud and clear, there will commonly be nothing but praise. Let this chapter be a testament to their value in the overall scheme of operatic things, to their individual and collective competencies, to their loyalty to their work and above all to their ability to keep a straight face under the most trying circumstances. And to their unerring instinct for observing, remembering and recounting the funny bits that none but they can know.

16

Very Friendly Friends

From the earliest days of the Intimate Opera Group, support bodies of spouses, relatives and friends have rallied around the singers, pianists, directors and designers who put the operas on the stage. While it was the artists' responsibility for ensuring that the shows went on, they could not have managed without their back-up teams. IOG was a do-it-yourself outfit – everybody bogged in to help with jobs like running front of house, begging and borrowing (if not actually stealing) props and costumes, setting out chairs before the show and stacking them up again after it. On tour there was even more to do; checking that the bus was booked, the piano tuned, all the gear and luggage loaded, organising and carrying out all the details for bumping in and out of church and school halls, institutes and other places where the ability to improvise was valued as highly as a beautiful voice.

Behind the front- and backstage workers was another phalanx.

As far as memories can determine, probably the first time that extra help was called on to raise funds for IOG was in 1961 after *The Turn of the Screw* left them with a debt of £800 – a huge amount for an amateur company. They were casual, to say the least, about money and relied on their members to cover costs. Laura Harrison recalled the Group running a series of fund-raising curry lunches. Such ad hoc rescues were entirely appropriate for the amateur – in the best sense of the word – ways of IOG, but once it was replaced by the professional New Opera South Australia in January 1973 something more formal was required.

At that time Friends organisations were rare, but they have since become integral to the successful running of performing arts companies, galleries, museums and libraries. They raise money, often in very large amounts, spread the work load among volunteers and, most importantly, allow non-experts to play an active, if peripheral, part in a field which they love but would never in a million years actually practise. But yet – what about those auctions where Friends raise lots of money by auctioning the rights to a walk-on part – remember surgeon and Sturt cricketer Donald Beard posing as a Philistine in the orgy scene in *Samson et Dalila*, playing Agamemnon to Marilyn Zschau's

Wendy Hopkins, Grant Smith and Brian Gilbertson, Friends' Introduction to *Fledermaus*, 1999

Elektra and coming back as her victim King Duncan in *Macbeth* – he says these thrilled him more than bowling Gary Sobers lbw twenty years earlier. (The umpire disallowed his appeal, saying that the punters had come to see Sobers bat, not Beard bowl.)

State Opera's Friends began with the New Opera Subscribers Committee in 1973. The earliest extant record is minutes of a meeting on 10 October. Mary Handley, a gifted pianist who had been accompanying IOG and New Opera since 1964 and was known as a musician who demanded high standards of herself and everyone she worked with and as an extremely capable organiser, was appointed Chairman. The members present were listed as Mrs Beinl, Mrs Ullett, Mrs Hunter and Mrs Jolly (Secretary). Apologies were recorded from Mrs Kidd, Mrs Taylor and Mrs S. Scott. The meeting noted that the company had 853 subscribers – a fine tally for a company not yet one year old – and that twenty of them would be invited to round up 80 people for a party 'at Mrs Handley's residence' on 30 November. Wine to be purchased from Pirramimma, members to make savouries.

The aims of the Committee were stated thus:

1 To keep subscribers
2 Selling subscriptions
3 Party bookings
4 Join in any company fund-raising
5 Welcoming and farewelling guest artists
6 Arranging receptions.

A bland comment that 'money would be available next year' can be taken, with hindsight, to indicate that negotiations were in train for sponsorship.

The members agreed that *pro tem* the Committee would be nominated by the NOSA Board, and that at its AGM they would hold their own election for a committee of ten members, some elected, some appointed by the Board. Very sensibly, they decided to draw up a constitution 'at a later date when the present committee has been functioning for a longer period'. Let's see how it works first – then formalise it.

Hidden subsidies from the medical profession must be acknowledged as an important source of background support for the companies IOG, New Opera and State Opera, and their friends and Friends. Kathleen Steele Scott's husband John, a prominent surgeon, was unstinting in his tolerance. Their home was base since the very beginnings for rehearsals, meetings, formal receptions, and informal (sometimes very informal) parties. Likewise for the Handleys. Harold, an ophthalmologist, seemed every bit as interested and involved in the company's doings as Mary, and cheerfully welcomed large numbers of committee members and party goers into his house and garden. Through it all, Kathleen and John brought up four children, Mary and Harold six.

In January 1974 the NOSA Board agreed that New Opera Subscribers' Committee should be established with a membership of ten, seven elected by the subscribers and three appointed by the Board.

This was a working group, dedicated to serving the company in many different ways. Minutes of meetings over the next two years reported that members had met visiting artists and seen them to their hotel rooms (with posies for the ladies and fruit juice for the men) to make them feel welcome. They organised lunches and receptions, found an ironing board for June Bronhill, lobbied local businesses to supply materials for the company at a discount and stood by to assist when New Opera entertained the Music Board and the Opera Board of the Australia Council, plus the AC Chairman H.C. (Nugget) Coombs, when their March meeting co-incided with the Adelaide Festival of Arts and New Opera's *The Excursions of Mr Broucek* in 1974. One of the Friends' best ideas was to initiate a lecture series leading up to each production, a practice started in 1974 and still going. And they were eminently practical. When Myer Fredman asked for help to furnish the new rehearsal rooms at Hilton, they supplied chairs, curtains, library shelving and wall hangings and cleared the overgrown garden.

The first mention of money was recorded in March 1975, when they agreed to ask New Opera for $50 to start them off. Thereafter, they hoped to be self-supporting. By May their sale of T-shirts proclaiming I LOVE NEW OPERA and adorned with the company's policy statement of Brünnhilde holding a broken spear had been so successful they were 'obliged to open a bank account'. The extent of their influence was reported to a meeting on 23 May. Requests that selected shops in prime positions – North Adelaide, Chesser Street – should exhibit costumes in their windows were frequently granted and in one case the owner asked for a display in the lead-up to *Così fan tutte* so that she could 'relate the opera to suitable evening dresses'. Stage designer Laurence Blake was to dress the window. This was serious business on both sides.

When the company changed its name to State Opera of SA in July 1976 the Subscribers Committee followed suit. At 10 am on 24 September they reported that the vacuum cleaner they had bought for the rehearsal rooms had been handed over to Russell Mitchell, State Opera's Planning Manager, dealt with other business, and without a hitch (the ground had obviously been well tilled) agreed to change their name to The Friends of The State Opera of South Australia. Elections followed, appointing Mrs Handley President, Mrs Steele Scott Vice President, Mrs Harrison Secretary, Miss Brokensha Treasurer (she handled the money matters with the utmost efficiency until her death in

John Tuckey, Thomas Edmonds and Elizabeth Campbell, Friends' Luncheon, 2000

December 1996) and Mrs Archer, Mrs Clark, Mrs Gallant, Mrs Mendels and Mrs Timms committee members. Thus the last meeting of the Subscribers' Committee melded with the first of the Friends'. Their proceedings were duly ratified by the Board of State Opera and on 17 April 1977, with Mr Vernon Lewis replacing Mrs Helen Clark, they were truly in business.

The range and inventiveness of their fund- and friend-raising functions was quite awesome – a Lyric Luncheon in the Crafers Institute and a family picnic with billy tea, bread and jam and a pie cart at the Angle Vale winery. Their bank account was so healthy in 1976 that they were able to assist with the costs of bringing Adrian Slack from the UK to take up the job of Director of Productions. To celebrate the success of *Midsummer Marriage* in the 1978 Adelaide Festival of Arts they ran a marriage feast at the Victoria Park race-course, serving barons of beef and 'Figaro', 'Traviata' and 'Rondine' salads ($8 per head – Friends $7, children $4).

When the Opera Theatre opened in February 1979 they took full advantage of its facilities. An information booth was set up in the foyer (and transferred to the Festival Theatre in 1989), the Board Room was annexed for meetings, the stage for dinners and the rehearsal room for a costume parade and sale. To show their gratitude for all this free accommodation they bought coffee urns for the dressing rooms.

By the time they celebrated their second birthday they had 1,000 members, more per capita than similar bodies in Melbourne and Sydney, and with the help of Richard Brown had secured funding from local builder AW Baulderstone, enabling them to produce and circulate a smart newsletter which persists to this day. Through this medium they have advertised their functions, promoted the company's productions, wooed new members and patrons, given space to members to report their opera visits outside Adelaide and run interviews with State Opera staff.

At their AGM in 1979 Mary Handley was re-elected chairman and Laura Harrison, a stalwart from IOG's beginnings in October 1957, stepped down as secretary. Dawn Wallace stepped up to take her place, not expecting to do the job for the next 24 years, as she has done.

In 1981 the Friends modified their constitution so that the president is elected for a one year term and may be re-elected for up to three years. The committee is re-elected each year, many of them serving for several terms.

As the Friends became more affluent, their usefulness to the company increased, and their efforts have added $300,000 to the company's coffers. They have sponsored productions – *Manon* 1985, *Sandrina's Secret* (1987), *Falstaff* (1995), *The Marriage of Figaro* (1997), the double bill (1998) and *Fledermaus* (1999). Among their many novel events was the dinner held on stage at the Festival Theatre on an off night during *Faust* in 1982 – 70 guests paid $20 to dine surrounded by the set and props of the opera. Their good example was followed by other organisations who recognised the vicarious thrill of treading the boards where the stars had been brightly shining only the night before. Their concerts were also novel. One report claimed that at their special concert in 1982 'singers danced, musical directors sang, and the general manager did both'.

In 1984 President Mary Archer invited Lillian Scott to set up and chair a Fund Raising Committee. With dramatically expanded horizons, they organised many financially productive functions over the following six years, some of them involving organisations outside the Friends. The most ambitious was the *Aida* Spectacular in 1990. With the collaboration of the Lady Mayoress's Committee and the Elizabethan Theatre Trust, the Friends rounded up decorative elephants from Carrick Hill, the Fourth Military District Band, the Adelaide University Choral Society, the Zanuba belly-dance troupe, jugglers, tumblers, stilt-walkers and Greenies for a grand display in the Masonic Hall. They attracted an audience of 300 at $65 a head and raised $20,000 for the Friends and selected local charities.

Their interest in and support for young singers has been unwavering. They contribute to the State Opera Aria prize within the Adelaide Eisteddfod, and in 1992 Dawn Wallace, Dorothy Timms and Doris Brokensha (replaced after her untimely death by Betty Ross) formed the 3 Ds Sunday Music Club to give emerging artists a platform and also raise money to help them with travel and study costs. Benefiting from this philanthropy have been Grant Doyle, Gisele Blanchard, Jacqueline Forster, Deborah Peake-Jones, Catriona Barr and Teresa La Rocca, all of them now either established in the profession or well on the way.

The Three Tenors – Philip Craig, Agim Hushi and Brian Gilbertson,
Stamford Grand, 1998

One of the Friends' most ambitious enterprises was the book *Through the Opera Glass* (1991) and its *Supplement* (1997). First mooted in 1985 by perpetual Friend Douglas Anders, and taken up by Charles Barnard, the idea was to assemble a register of all operas performed in South Australia since settlement in 1836. Edited by musicologist Robyn Holmes with linking sections written by Anders and financed by Kathleen Steele Scott, the books were solidly supported by the Friends, who carried out the arduous and often tedious leg work of collecting data from libraries, performing arts collections, private memorabilia and any other source they could plunder. Details are given of all the operas and music theatre pieces, with their composers, conductors, production teams, dates, venues and performers. It was a huge task and has proved invaluable as a source of basic information for any further research, such as was needed for this history of State Opera. The achievement was recognised in 1991 by the award of Outstanding Resources Project by Opera Guilds International in Kansas City. The submission was prepared by Jill McGorman, Friend, and sister of Dawn Wallace. In 1998, the same body presented a second accolade to the Friends under its Partners in Excellence plan for continuous operation for over 21 years.

Stephen Phillips and Dawn Wallace drawing the prize in questionnaire lottery, 2000

The Friends' support was a vital factor in the success of State Opera's *Ring* cycle in 1998, and the work of committee members Peter Bassett and Lillian Scott is acknowledged in detail in the *Ring* section of this book.

Through their 25 years, the Friends have never had problems with filling positions as office bearers and committee members. So highly respected is their organisation that members actually compete for positions and in most recent years formal elections have had to be held. Many of their chairmen have been well respected in their own professions and fields, and also active in other areas of the opera company's operations. Mary Handley chaired the Friends from inception in 1977 to 1981 and was appointed to the State Opera Board in 1982, where she served for another eight years. In 1997 her invaluable services were recognised with the award of OAM. Transition from Friends chairmanship to State Opera Board membership was also made by Pamela Mendels (1981), Lillian Scott (1990) and Christopher Stone (1997). The full list of the Friends' admirable leaders serving for either two or three years each is completed by Mary Archer (1984), Laura Harrison (1987 and playing a part in the whole story from 1957), Mary Rose Collom (1992) and Julie David (1994).

At the AGM in April 2000 John Tuckey was elected president, Kay Walsh and Jan Grant first and second vice presidents, Dawn Wallace secretary, Yvonne McMurray treasurer and Fay Haddad minute secretary. Eleven members were elected to the committee, which includes the company's general director ex officio. The treasurer reported a bank balance of $23,000.

Dawn Wallace was honoured for her long and dedicated services to the Friends by being made a Life Member of the State Opera of South Australia in July 2000.

Continuity of people and principles has been at the core of the Friends and a major source of their vitality. Apart from those already saluted in this chapter, two people merit special acknowledgement. Kathleen Steele Scott was an original Subscribers Committee and Board member and tireless in her moral and practical support all her days. Among many other things, she wrote reports for many years to the national journal *Opera Australia* and its successors informing the whole country of the latest concert, the latest lunch (on a boat, at a winery, on stage, with Joan Sutherland, John Pringle or June Bronhill as guest of honour) and making it clear that the Friends were all having a marvellous time and raising lots of money with it. In 1984 she was awarded an AM, and in 1992 was honoured with the Dame Joan Hammond Medal, both of them for her outstanding achievements on behalf of music generally and opera in particular.

Richard Brown, founding chairman of NOSA, served for a total of twelve years in different capacities, notably as the Friends' nominee on the company

Major sponsors 1999–2000

Government
of South Australia

Council of Benefactors 2000

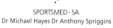

State Opera sponsors as at December 2000

board – his appointment was proof positive that he was trusted to the absolute maximum by both bodies for his integrity and his clearsighted concern for the whole business of opera in South Australia. At the time of writing the Friends are flourishing, proud of a membership of 800 and gearing up for *Parsifal* in 2001 and a new *Ring* in 2004.

Besides the Friends, State Opera has gradually assembled two more cohorts of friends who have supported the company in good times and bad, and have often been the vital factor in bad times becoming good.

An important agent in the turnaround in the company's fortunes from an accumulated deficit of over one million dollars in 1988 to around $250,000 in 1993 was that many of the productions over the five years since the desperate financial situation had become public knowledge were supported by sponsors. This fact in itself is testament to the persuasive powers of Hugh Cunningham, Ian D. Campbell, Ian Johnston and Bill Gillespie. Programs from as early as 1977 carry paid advertisements from Elders Lensworth Finance, a gesture of financial support which gradually developed into more overt forms such as the generous funding from the *Advertiser*, which created huge public interest in the opening of the Opera Theatre in 1979. During Ian Johnston's tenure the State Government Insurance Commission (SGIC) with premises adjoining the company in Market Street in the city became a significant supporter. By 1982 the company had succeeded in persuading businesses to sponsor individual productions – Bank of New South Wales for *Così fan tutte*, long time loyal supporter Lensworth Finance for *The Tales of Hoffmann*; Leighton Holdings took on *Aida* in 1985 and SGIC *The Flying Dutchman* and *The Italian Girl in Algiers* in 1986. By 1993 SOSA was over its troubles and sufficiently stabilised to attract new sponsors – Commonwealth Bank (*Macbeth*), BHP, 5AD and Singapore Airlines (*Carmen*). Sponsorship of individual singers, conductors and instruments (the Wagner tubas) began with *The Ring*, when more than twenty patrons covered the costs of selected artists and equipment.

Pre-eminent among the individual philanthropists have been Mrs Diana Ramsay AO and the late Mr James Ramsay AO, whose funding of the costs of surtitles began in 1989 and has enabled thousands of patrons to understand what was going on, and hundreds of performers to enjoy being understood – especially in the funny bits. And since August the company has been supported by the Thora and Frank Pearce Opera Foundation, whose funds are to be used exclusively for cultural purposes associated with opera.

At the time of writing, and at least from 1996, productions have carried the name of a major sponsor, including the Friends, and to the above list should be added Western Mining Corporation, Boral, Qantas, Clipsal, Santos, Arthur Andersen and P&O Nedlloyd. Of course their money is crucial to State Opera's survival, but their support means more than mere dollars. In many cases their employees are able to attend operas at discount rates, thus spreading knowledge and appreciation of the art form through communities that would otherwise be difficult to reach, and when Arthur Andersen turned on champagne for the whole audience during the interval of *Romeo et Juliette*'s première in April 2000 State Opera revelled in the illusion that it was actually living in the way to which it would dearly love to become accustomed. This sort of generosity is not entirely altruistic, but it's as near to it as we are likely to come.

The program for *Tosca*, the last opera reported on in this book, includes a page displaying, with obvious pride as well as heartfelt gratitude, the names and logos of six major sponsors, including the arts agencies of both state and commonwealth governments, and a further sixteen under the heading of Council of Benefactors 2000 who are 'dedicated to raising financial support for the company by way of benefaction, sponsorship and special events.' Also acknowledged are more than 120 patrons, including a sizeable number from outside South Australia attracted by the company's enterprises, who donate amounts varying from $50 to over $2000.

Highly trained and carefully selected staff members of opera companies all over the world, and especially in Australia where the tradition of government subsidy is stronger than that of corporate and private donations, work with great diligence and even greater tact persuading senior executives of large companies and philanthropically minded individuals that giving money to support opera is an investment, just like buying shares. There would be a handsome return – not of money, but something much more valuable – helping the most noble, the most sophisticated of all artforms to flourish, assisting in the creation of more and better productions, nurturing young singers who would be the internationally acclaimed Toscas, Mimis, Scarpias and Rigolettos in the next ten or twenty years.

From the beginnings of New Opera SA to the present, the company's best mate has been the government of SA through the agency of its Department of the Arts. From the $15,000 which got New Opera started in 1973 to the grant of $1.7 million (including opera services from the ASO) listed in the 1999 Annual Report, State Opera could not have survived even in the good times, let alone the bad, without official support. During the financial crises of 1988 the state's politicians could have closed the company down by the simple expedient of refusing funds. Instead, cabinet agreed with the arts minister, John Bannon, that no self-respecting state, especially one with claims to the title of arts capital of Australia, could afford to be without an opera company. It was a basic principle, leading to the bailout that enabled SOSA to recover its equilibrium and re-build itself into the thriving organisation of today. Don Dunstan, Murray Hill, John Bannon, Anne Lévy and Diana Laidlaw – opera in South Australia owes its current financial and artistic security to the fact that successive politicians with the arts in their portfolios were not only fans of opera but believed that it plays a major role in the state's culture.

Good friends are worth their weight in gold.

17

Postlude

❧

Early in 2000, another dazzling announcement was made by the company that had dared to put on *The Ring* ahead of its elders in the national company. The first Australian fully staged production of Wagner's *Parsifal* would be mounted in Adelaide in September 2001. Written (both words and music) in 1882, one year before the death of the composer, *Parsifal* was his last and most ambitious opera, and a natural choice for a company bent on consolidating its claim both to Wagner and to major premières. With engagements confirmed for *Ring* conductor Jeffrey Tate, a powerful cast led by distinguished Danish heldentenor Poul Elming who first took on the hugely demanding lead role in Bayreuth in 1992, a number of outstanding Australian singers and director Elke Neidhardt, State Opera was able to put the seal on the enterprise when F.H. Faulding and Co Limited agreed to assume naming rights for the *Parsifal* season.

But the company learnt a lesson from 1998 that their subscribers divide into pro- and anti-Wagnerites, and offers substantial inducements to the latter in 2001. Following its nose in the theory that collaborations with other arts organisations will attract new audiences (and please the government), SOSA planned a national premiere of *Sacred and Profane*, with the Australian Ballet dancing to the Fauré *Requiem* and Orff's *Carmina Burana*; the Verdi *Requiem* in concert – all calling on the Adelaide Philharmonia Chorus – a new production (their last was in 1975) of *The Turn of the Screw* and a new production of *Andrea Chénier*. And of course, *Parsifal*.

2001 will be a crucial testing time as will 2004, when the Australian-built *Ring* currently in embryo will come around.

The history of State Opera so far, 1957 to 2000, reports fluctuating fortunes, many brilliant successes, and a few dismal failures, but its trajectory has managed to maintain its upward direction overall. As long as gifted and dedicated administrators and staff can be found to run the business; outstanding singers, conductors, directors and designers can be enticed to grace the stages; enthusiastic, public spirited and preferably (but not necessarily) prominent persons are willing to chair and sit on the Board; philanthropists continue to make major investments; and as long as the governments of the day believe that an opera company is an essential component of any modern state, there is no reason why the State Opera of South Australia, celebrating its 25th anniversary in 2001, should not deliver more of the best of the same for another 25 years. And another. And another . . .

$\mathscr{A}$ppendix

Administrators

IOG	John Worthley (de facto)		1957
	Kathleen Steele Scott	President	1960
NOSA	Justin Macdonnell	Administrator	1973
SOSA	Ian D. Campbell	General Manager	1976
	Larry Ruffell	General Manager	1982
	Andrew Pain	Acting December–April	1983–4
	Ian Johnston	General Manager	1984
	Justin Macdonnell	Acting April-June	1988
	William Gillespie	General Manager	1988
		General Director	1991
	Stephen Phillips	General Director	1995

Musical Directors

NOSA	Barry Golding	Resident Conductor and Principal Coach	1974
	Myer Fredman	Musical Director	1975
SOSA	Myer Fredman	Musical Director	1976
	Denis Vaughan	Musical Director	1981
	Alexander Ingram	Musical Director	1985
	Andrew Greene	Musical Director	1986
	David Kram	Musical Director	1987

Board Chairmen

NOSA	Richard Brown	1973
	Hugh Cunningham	1974
SOSA	Hugh Cunningham	1976
	Kevin Miller	1981
	Graham Prior	1982
	David Tonkin	1985
	Alan Hodgson	1986
	Keith Smith	1988
	Timothy O'Loughlin	1994
	Colin Dunsford	1997

References

Bebbington, W. (ed.) *The Oxford Companion to Australian Music*, Oxford University Press, 1997

Campbell, L. *By Popular Demand*, Wakefield Press, 1998

Edgeloe, V. *The Language of Human Feeling*, University of Adelaide, 1984

Holden, A. (ed.) *The Penguin Opera Guide*, Viking, 1995

Holmes, R. (ed.) *Through the Opera Glass*, The Friends of State Opera, 1991

Through the Opera Glass: A Supplement, The Friends of State Opera, 1997

Linn, R. Oral History of Intimate Opera Group, unpublished

McCredie, A. (ed.) *From Colonel Light into the Footlights*, Pagel, 1988

Sadie, S. (ed.) *The New Grove Dictionary of Music and Musicians*, Macmillan, 1980

Sadie, S. (ed.) *The New Grove Dictionary of Opera*, Macmillan, 1998

Salter, E. *Daisy Bates*, Corgi Books, 1973

Scholes, P. (ed.) *The Oxford Companion to Music*, Oxford University Press, 1955

Ward, P. *A Singular Act*, Wakefield Press, 1992

Sources

Adelaide *Advertiser*

Adelaide Review

Melbourne *Age*

Bulletin

Flinders University Library

Messenger Press

Mortlock Library

News

Opera (London)

Opera News (New York)

Opera Australia 1978

Opera Australasia 1994

Opera-Opera 1997

Performing Arts Collection

State Library of SA

Adelaide *Sunday Mail*

Sydney Morning Herald

*A*cknowledgements

Len Amadio AM
Douglas Anders
Robert Angove
ArtSA
Peter Bleby
Board of State Opera of SA
Richard Brown
Rae Cocking
Margaret Cunningham
Hugh Cunningham
Robert Dawe OAM
Kate Deller-Evans
Decie Denholm
Michael Deves
Dymocks Booksellers
   Burnside Village
Thomas Edmonds AM
Alan Farwell

David Farwell
Melanie Fechner
Flinders University
   Professor Faith Trent
   Professor Graham
   Tulloch
   Professor Alan Russell
Kay Gallant
Judy Gibb
Julie Glazbrook
David Gyger
Mary Handley OAM
William Harrison
Laura Harrison
Fiona Hemstock
David Lowe
Justin Macdonnell
Margaret Oates

Jeffrey Oates
Geoffrey Partington
Dean Patterson
Jo Peoples
David Perry
Stephen Phillips
Lyndon Piddington
Rodney Pike
Diana Ramsay AO
Keith Smith
David Symon
Judith Symon
Kathleen Steele
   Scott AM
Phillip Virgo
Dawn Wallace
David Wilson
John Worthley

Index